Chris Kronner has dedicated his creative energy, professional skills, and a lifetime of burger experiences to understanding America's favorite sandwich. In *A Burger to Believe In*, this trusted chef reveals the secrets behind his art and obsession, and teaches you how to create all of the elements of a perfect burger at home. Including tips for sourcing and grinding high-quality meat, musings on what makes a good bun, creative ideas for toppings (spoiler alert: there are more bad ideas out there than good, and restraint is the name of the game), and more than forty burger accompaniments and alternatives—from superior onion rings to seasonal salads to Filet-O-Fish-inspired Crab Burgers—this book is not only a burger bible, but also a meditation on creating perfection in simplicity.

A BURGER
TO BELIEVE IN

A BURGER
TO BELIEVE IN

RECIPES AND FUNDAMENTALS

CHRIS KRONNER
WITH PAOLO LUCCHESI

PHOTOGRAPHY BY ERIC WOLFINGER

TEN SPEED PRESS
California | New York

Contents

Foreword

By Daniel Duane, journalist and author

Like all home cooks, I have my gurus—master chefs living on the pages of their own cookbooks, always ready to guide my hand. Thomas Keller whispers through his *Bouchon* cookbook that if I pat dry my whole raw chickens and salt heavily before roasting, I'll get crispy skin and juicy breast-meat. David Chang, through his *Momofuku* cookbook, keeps my ramen on point while Alice Waters, in *Chez Panisse Vegetables*, knows exactly what I should do with everything I just bought at the farmer's market.

Chris Kronner is not yet a household name, but he will be when everybody discovers why Chris has been my personal burger guru for so many years. I made lots of burgers before I met Chris, and I even made burgers with ambition. I tried country bread instead of buns, arugula instead of iceberg, Sriracha mayo instead of ketchup. I even made a few burgers I liked. But I never made a burger I loved, and I certainly never made a burger that satisfied my daughters.

Then came the fateful night that my wife took me to a pop-up called Kronnerburger, at a seedy bar in San Francisco's Mission District. I'll never forget the sight of that aluminum tray appearing in front of me, bearing a burger so strict in its classicism that it looked like the burger Andy Warhol would have painted if he'd been dreaming Dairy Queen instead of Campbell's Soup. I'll never forget that first bite, either, the savory umami of charred rare beef fusing with sharply acid pickle and sweet griddled onion and mayo enriched with vintage cheddar—on a bun at once tender and sweet and firm and neither too small nor too large. That bite taught me that I knew nothing about hamburgers, and that somebody in the kitchen knew everything, and that my personal happiness depended upon remedying the imbalance.

Chris worked for years in serious San Francisco restaurant kitchens as what they call "muscle," one of those unsung heroes who lets restaurant owners sleep at night by guaranteeing that every dish comes out right, every time. Along the way, Chris cooked so many tens of thousands of first-rate burgers for so many delighted customers that he developed a bone-deep appreciation for the fact that a classic American burger is one of the culinary world's few perfect things—like Texas barbecue, pizza marinara, and buttermilk fried chicken. Put another way, Chris came to see that a classic American burger cannot be improved by the addition of silliness like teriyaki-glazed pineapple and

Canadian bacon, or guacamole and sour cream, much less fancy bread and Sriracha mayo. A classic American burger can only be improved by perfecting each and every one of the classic elements—beef, bun, tomato, pickle, lettuce, condiment—without making them into something else, and by then combining those elements in precisely the right proportions.

The book you are holding is the end result of Chris's long and successful quest to do exactly that—both in his fantastic Oakland restaurant, Kronnerburger, which is by far the greatest burger joint in Northern California, and in the testing of these recipes. Lucky enough to be along for the ride, I have tried every one of Chris's innovations, right on down to the dry-aging of grass-fed beef chuck in a mini-fridge in my own basement. I have tried them so many times, with such glorious results, that my daughters named our kitten "Kronner" and have not asked me to make burgers in years. Instead, they have learned to say, "Dad, will you make Kronnerburgers tonight?" So I speak from experience when I say that accepting Chris Kronner into your life, and embracing The Way of The Kronnerburger, will transform your own burgers into what you've always wanted them to be, even if you didn't quite know it: sacramental celebrations of the Great American Sandwich.

Preamble

There is no perfect.

The hamburger is possibly America's most recognizable and representative food. What started as the most democratic, wholesome square meal meant to be consumed quickly for a fair price has mutated into forms unrecognizable to those original burger salesmen, not to mention the ranchers who raised the beef. Since the hamburger's creation, it has followed the revolutions and undulations of farming and economics in this country. Its path—and current forms—cannot be separated from the divergent systems of farming and animal rearing in the United States. On one extreme, there is the fast-food hamburger. Like the corporate industrial farms of which it is a product, it champions speed, quantity, and a price only achievable through subsidies and methods that compromise taste, animals, land, and the people involved in the systems that produce and consume it. On the other side is the well-intentioned, but often fetishized, higher-end product, which places importance on better values but struggles to make its product financially viable and accessible to the masses.

I have eaten a thousand hamburgers. Hamburgers made of young beef, old beef, dry-aged beef, wet-aged beef, goose, wild boar, venison. Hamburgers made of A5 Kobe, water buffalo, plant-based "meat," brown bear (also made into burritos), elk, prosciutto. And hamburgers made of the crummiest, grayest, unidentifiably sad meat imaginable.

I have eaten hamburgers in cars, restaurants, backyards, ballparks, and the woods; on trains and boats; at the movies and the entrance to Machu Picchu; in Denver, Atlanta, Asheville, Seattle, Portland, Nashville, New York, New Orleans, Los Angeles, Detroit, London, Paris, Beirut, Istanbul, Buenos Aires, Vancouver, Montevideo, Mexico City, Lyon, Tokyo; and everywhere in between.

I have cooked close to a billion hamburgers, mostly in restaurants, many at home, on grills, in microwaves, in alleys, in a couple of museums, on rooftops, in art galleries, in parking lots, and in fields next to said hamburger's still-grazing brethren.

I have looked a cow in its eyes before putting a bullet between them. I have seen cows birthed and watched them die.

What is presented in the following pages is the result of a lot of burger cooking and burger eating. With this book, I originally set out with very specific intentions, to write about the ONE way to make ONE burger using ONE very specific type of beef only. That was dumb. I am dumb. What I found, as Paolo and I dove deeper, is that there are many ways to make a better burger, in the choices you make both in your purchases and preparations.

Before and during the process of writing of this book, I tried as many types of beef as possible. I also explored as many variations of burger cooking as possible. I have talked burgers and beef with meat salespeople, burger eaters, fancy chefs, line cooks, and beef ranchers of many stripes. We very likely missed some points of view and more than a few closely guarded burger secrets. Maybe your dad cooks burgers over an old, abandoned well full of smoldering tires and lit fireworks. Maybe your grandmother swears by a burger ratio of 80 percent beef, 5 percent French onion soup mix, and 15 percent lean hawk meat. I fully respect your hamburger traditions.

The beef that I find to be best, in my home of Northern California, may not be available to you. Depending on where you live and cook, use the best of what is available, the ingredients you like the most. If you have access to lovingly raised animals that you can see from your driveway, you are very lucky. If you have the ability to dry-age beef and bake bread, you are very lucky. If you can't go shake hands with the steer you eat and don't have desire or space to slowly dry-age your meat, don't worry, because we have useful burger information for every level of interest and devotion.

There is no "perfect," but there *is* bad. Bad should be avoided if possible. (Trust me on this one.)

I have watched hamburgers be eaten by the very young and very old, by cowboys and vegans, by beautiful women and equally beautiful boys, mostly resulting in smiles and elation, occasionally total revulsion.

Which hamburger was the best? Almost all of them.

You have eaten hamburgers, too. At least one. You may have even enjoyed it. What did it taste like?

This book is for you.

HOW TO COOK
A HAMBURGER

Thoughtful reductive simplicity: A hamburger is the sum of its parts. Don't complicate it. Start with the best parts. If the best parts aren't available, allow the parts you have to shine by treating them thoughtfully.

Decades ago, Dean Martin famously shared his burger recipe. It's a simple one. Start with a pound of ground beef and two ounces of chilled bourbon. Preheat a heavy frying pan over medium-high heat and lightly sprinkle in some table salt. Handling lightly, form the meat into four patties, add to the pan, and cook for about 4 minutes on each side. Pour the chilled bourbon into a chilled shot glass and serve the meat and bourbon on a TV tray.

In reality, Mr. Martin's burger is probably pretty gross and suitable mainly for middle-aged alcoholics who need some sort of fuel to keep the whiskey quiet while they stare into the void as reruns of *The Colgate Comedy Hour* play at full volume. At the same time, Mr. Martin was pretty close to achieving the perfect burger recipe. Especially in one elemental way: its simplicity.

There is no one way to cook or compose a hamburger. Use the best beef you can. Salt it liberally. Cook it on a hot surface. Get your favorite toppings and put everything between two halves of a bun. Eat it all, as soon as you can.

That's the beauty of a hamburger. At its core, it belongs to everyone, home cook and restaurant chef alike. Nearly everyone cooks—and can cook—burgers at home. Burgers are equally comfortable at parties as they are providing solace to the lonely solo diner. They are personal, customizable, democratic, and deeply interwoven into our shared food memory.

What follows is the Kronnerburger recipe, in its simplest form.

A Burger for One

Form 5 ounces of ground beef into a patty that is 4 inches wide and 1 inch thick. Salt both sides well.

Evenly butter the cut sides of a bun. Toast the bun, buttered side down, in a pan over medium-low heat, until golden brown and softened through.

If cooking over a grill, heat grill to high heat. Reduce heat to medium and put your patty on the grill. Cook for 2 minutes over medium heat, flip once, and cook for another minute, until the beef is cooked rare.

If cooking on a stove top, heat a cast-iron skillet over high heat. When the pan is hot, spread ½ teaspoon of butter on one side of the patty. Cook the patty for 2 minutes on one side to get some good crusty caramelization. Flip and cook 1 minute more until the beef is cooked rare.

Place the patty on the toasted bottom bun. Top with pickles, a thin ring of red onion, a leaf or two of cold lettuce, and a slice or two of tomato (if in season). Give the top bun a smear of mayonnaise. Eat immediately.

A Brief but Thrilling Note on How to Use This Book

There is no one way to cook anything, especially a burger. The goal of this book is provide ways to make your favorite burger better, no matter your level of skill or ambition.

Extremely Lazy: Just look at the photos and have burgers delivered.

Slightly Less Useless: Buy everything premade and combine into burgers.

Vaguely Interested: Skim book and use some of the techniques—steam-toasting buns, buying better beef—to make the most of store-bought ingredients.

Ambitious: Become friends with your local butcher and buy freshly ground dry-aged beef. Make quick pickles. Buy locally baked buns. Make cheddar mayo. Spend an inordinate amount of time choosing the perfect tomato.

Really, Really Dedicated: Build a small dry-aging chamber, dry-age your beef, bake your own buns, make all other ingredients from scratch. Scream at family or roommates about how they don't appreciate anything.

Fervent Acolyte: Start a farming commune committed to reversing desertification through multispecies grazing. Grow wheat, lettuce, tomatoes, onions, and cucumbers. Raise a dairy herd and use its milk to make cheddar cheese. After five to twelve years, kill part of the herd and dry-age their carcasses. Harvest and mill the wheat to make flour for buns. Build a forge. Fabricate a grill. Cook burgers for the rest of the cult.

This book is an exploration of the stages of burger obsession, for every level of cook. The Kronnerburger itself relies on four constants:

- **It is made with grass-fed dairy beef.**
- **The beef has been dry-aged for a minimum of thirty days.**
- **The beef has been freshly ground.**
- **The beef has been cooked over a wood fire.**

In the following chapter, we'll discuss each of these components and lay out the processes for each in painstakingly delicious detail. The end result is an ambitious, but worthwhile, master class in burgers.

That said, even implementing one of the four—or any of the other, smaller components, from grilling onions to roasting bone marrow—will improve your burger game at home. If you're a real go-getter and want to learn how to grind your own burger meat or pickle some pig skin, this book will explain everything you need to know about those projects. But if you just want to cook yourself a quick weeknight burger, asking your friendly butcher to grind some grass-fed chuck for you is a mighty fine shortcut.

The same goes for condiments. Yes, you can make your own spicy Calabrian Chile Mayonnaise like on page 216—or you can mix some chopped hot peppers into your favorite store-bought mayo.

The basic properties of a hamburger allow anyone, at any cooking skill level, to create one. This book is all about opting in on any level.

SIMPLE WAYS TO
DO BURGERS BETTER

- **Choose the best meat.** My ideal beef is freshly ground, organic, pasture-raised chuck from a dairy cow that has been dry-aged. Admittedly, not something you would find at a gas station or the Piggly Wiggly. Seek it out. Alternatively, fresh ground, grass-fed chuck is more readily available. If it is dry-aged, all the better. When using grass-fed beef, fattier is better. Generally speaking, 80 percent lean to 20 percent fat is a good ratio; 70 percent is better for grass-fed. Try choosing a whole piece of beef and grinding it; any butcher will grind it for you. If you choose this route, make sure the butcher doesn't trim and discard the fat. Trust me, freshly ground beef may change the way you think about hamburgers.

- **Don't choose the worst meat.** Avoid any ground beef that is frozen, or has ever been frozen. Ground meat is 70 percent water. Freezing can cause cellular ruptures, leading to moisture loss during cooking. Basically, your meat deflates and shrivels up. Prepacked ground trim is generally ground into a paste because the stuff that goes into it probably wouldn't resemble food for humans if left in larger pieces.

- **Shape your beef.** Handle the ground beef as minimally as possible from the grinder to the grill. I like to form the ground beef into disks using a 4-inch ring mold. Put a small sheet of plastic wrap over the ring mold and, using your palm, gently press the portioned ground beef into the mold. The meat should be firmly packed and evenly distributed. Pop the patty out with the plastic wrap and put onto a baking sheet. Refrigerate until ready to cook.

- **Salt your burger.** The balance of salt and fat is crucial. Immediately before cooking, liberally coat both sides of the patty with salt, about ½ teaspoon on each side.

- **Buy decent buns.** Great buns are not too large, not too dry, not too fatty, and soft yet sturdy enough to stand up to your burger. If you're shopping at a grocery store with limited options, opt for the old-fashioned American-style white-bread buns, with or without sesame seeds.

HELPFUL EQUIPMENT

Hand or electric grinder,
for grinding meat

Scale, for portioning meat
(and weighing bun ingredients)

4-inch ring mold, for molding
perfect patties

Good cast-iron skillet, for cooking
perfect patties

Food processor, for making mayo
and sauces

Wood-fired grill, for cooking

High-temperature thermometer,
for frying safely

(And if your only option is an oversize brioche bun, cut out ½ to 1 inch from the middle and reserve for something else.) Either way, a crusty or bready bun doesn't work very well. The bread shouldn't be more difficult to bite through than the patty itself. Always remember, even toasted white bread is better than a ciabatta roll. If you doubt this, ask the folks at Louis' Lunch in New Haven, Connecticut, the birthplace of the "hamburger sandwich."

- **Optimize the bun-to-meat ratio.** Again, balance. Two proportionally balanced burgers are better than one massive burger. Don't listen to what the fake food news tells you. A good rule of thumb: The thickness of each bun half should be roughly equal to that of the uncooked patty.

- **Steam-toast your buns.** It's always good to toast your buns. It's even better to simultaneously steam them . . . with butter. Butter the cut sides of the bun with room-temperature whole butter.

Place them, buttered side down, on a flat surface (like a skillet or griddle) and toast over medium-low heat until lightly browned. Not only does this create a nice exterior crust but the moisture in the milk solids from the butter turns to steam, which rises and helps soften the bun. This method comes in particularly handy when using not-fresh bread that may need a little resuscitation. Covering the pan can help as well. For especially dry bread, add a little bit of water to the hot pan to create additional steam when covered.

- **Don't use tongs.** When cooking, turn the burgers with a spatula. Or if you're supercool and tough—or have congenital analgesia—use your hands, aka God's spatula. A spatula allows easy flipping and won't break the patty in half. To practice burger flippery, so you can impress guests at your barbecue this summer, we recommend urinal pucks or English muffins as stand-ins for actual burger patties.

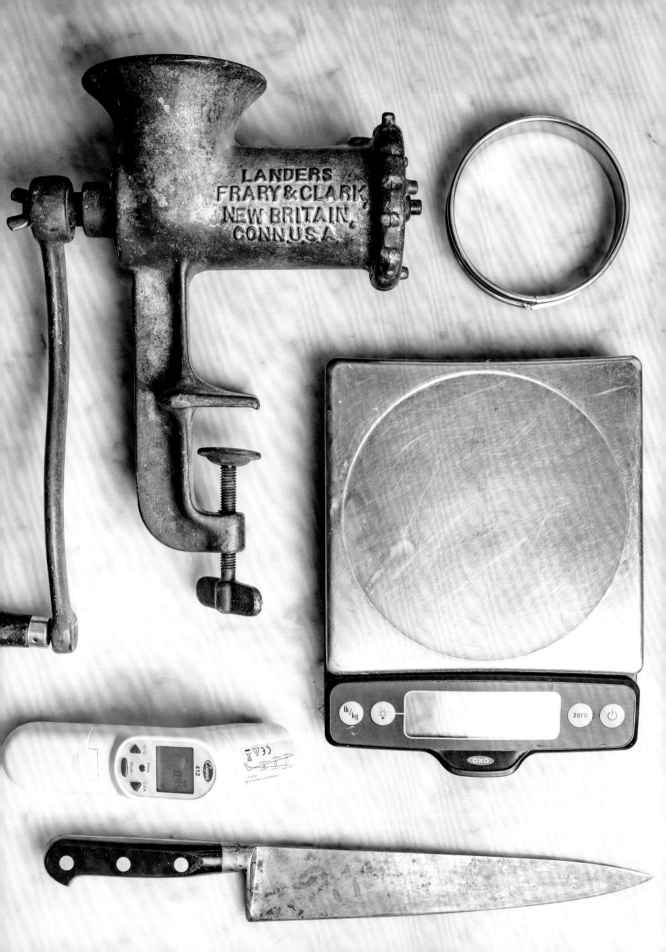

COWS AND BEEF AND BURGERS COWS AND BEEF AND BURGERS
COWS AND BEEF AND BURGERS COWS AND BEEF AND BURGER
COWS AND BEEF AND BURGERS COWS AND BEEF AND BURGERS
COWS AND BEEF AND BURGERS COWS AND BEEF AND BURGERS
COWS AND BEEF AND BURGERS COWS AND BEEF AND BURGERS
COWS AND BEEF AND BURGERS COWS AND BEEF AND BURGER
COWS AND BEEF AND BURGERS COWS AND BEEF AND BURGER
COWS AND BEEF AND BURGERS COWS AND BEEF AND BURGER
COWS AND BEEF AND BURGERS COWS AND BEEF AND BURGERS
COWS AND BEEF AND BURGERS COWS AND BEEF AND BURGER
COWS AND BEEF AND BURGERS COWS AND BEEF AND BURGER
COWS AND BEEF AND BURGERS COWS AND BEEF AND BURGER

CHAPTER ONE

COWS
AND
BEEF
AND
BURGERS

COWS AND BEEF AND BURGERS   COWS AND BEEF AND BURGE
COWS AND BEEF AND BURGERS   COWS AND BEEF AND BURGE
COWS AND BEEF AND BURGERS   COWS AND BEEF AND BURG
COWS AND BEEF AND BURGERS   COWS AND BEEF AND BURGE
COWS AND BEEF AND BURGERS   COWS AND BEEF AND BURGE
COWS AND BEEF AND BURGERS   COWS AND BEEF AND BURGE

A BURGER TO SAVE THE WORLD

What would happen if you spent a decade, or a life, focused on creating your personal best version of one thing?

The Kronnerburger has been more than a decade in the making. That sounds a little silly to say out loud, especially with the name, but it's true. That's not to say it's taken me ten years to figure out how to form ground meat into circles—that would not be a good use of time. But this burger has been a constant evolution, the result of a relentless, often obsessive and quixotic quest for the perfect American burger. It is not topped with foie gras, lobster, and gold leaf; it is the backyard burger of our dreams. Kronnerburger, the restaurant and the sandwich, are driven by a pursuit of simplicity (with detours).

Where will you start?

Start with the core components. And the primary component of a burger? It's the beef. So we'll start with the beef.

The idea of making a burger to improve the world only makes sense if we first understand why the world needs improving.

On an elemental, almost primitive level, there's a symbiotic relationship between cows and humans. Humans raise, feed, and care for cows, protecting them from predators. In return, cows have evolved to turn grass, which humans can't eat, into meat that humans can eat. Yet beef is one of the most resource-intensive food sources on the planet. As such, the sustainability discussion surrounding beef is something much, much different than the sustainability of fish or the sustainability of tomatoes.

The United States is the world's largest producer of beef. In 2015, American beef production was 23.7 billion pounds, according to the U.S. Department of Agriculture (USDA). The total amount of beef consumed by Americans was nearly 25 billion pounds in that same calendar year, which computes to about 78 pounds of beef per person. That is nearly a quarter pound per person per *day*.

Over the first fifteen years of the twenty-first century, American beef consumption has decreased, which is a good thing. However, global consumption is up and is expected to keep rising. Meanwhile, the profit generated by the beef industry has skyrocketed, from $60 billion in 2002 to $105 billion in 2015. (Again, those are USDA numbers.)

Long story short, beef is big business in America, and for the foreseeable future it will continue to be.

In 2011, methane from livestock accounted for 39 percent of all the greenhouse gas emissions from agriculture, according to a report from the Food and Agriculture Organization of the United Nations. That's more than from synthetic fertilizer or deforestation. Methane from livestock rose 11 percent between 2001 and 2011. The bulk of the emissions—55 percent—came from beef cattle. Dairy cows, buffalo, sheep, and goats accounted for the rest.

The environmental problems go beyond the well-publicized emissions, too. Manure from industrial production causes water pollution. Monoculture crops are grown and promoted for feed. Water consumption is significant. (To be honest, the list of worrisome environmental grievances against the industrial cattle system could fill up another book, but then we wouldn't have room for that biscuit recipe, and they told us this was supposed to be a cookbook.)

But there are silver linings within the environmental train wreck. When it comes to grass-fed beef, according to a seminal 2017 grass-fed beef study by the Stone Barns Center for Food and Agriculture, regenerative grazing can be good for the land, having been shown to increase soil organic matter, soil fertility, and water-holding capacity. Also, early studies have also shown that regenerative grazing techniques with grass-fed cows can encourage carbon sequestration.

The vast majority of American beef, roughly 80 percent, comes from four large corporations. This is insane. The cows are raised on feedlots—fenced-in compounds where tens of thousands of cows, if not more, live shoulder to shoulder, ankle-deep in their own shit.

When the feedlot cows reach a weight where the feed they're given no longer results in the desired return of fat, usually at a little over a year old, they go to slaughter. It is a quick, sad, sedentary life, one without physical activity or much regard for the cow's health or cleanliness or well-being or planetary contribution beyond a cheap source of protein. USDA studies have also found that grain feed can increase the probability of health and digestive problems for the cows; grass, on the other hand, is their natural source of food.

Here's the other thing: grain-fed beef doesn't taste like much. Animals taste like what they eat. A cow that is getting pumped full of homogenized feed designed to get it as plump as can be—as quickly as possible—will carry that flavor, or lack thereof. Industrial beef tastes one-dimensional, uniformly fatty and bland because that is exactly how its production is designed. It may be predictable and satiate you in an elemental way, but it doesn't taste like anything.

Compared to the flavors of its feedlot counterpart, grass-fed beef is the Technicolor version, though even with its growing popularity, it still occupies a tiny fraction of the beef market. According to Nielsen data, retail sales of labeled fresh grass-fed beef have doubled every year from 2012 to 2016,

but it still consists of less than 10 percent of the overall market.

In a not-too-distant past, I spent some time living on a beef ranch in a rural county in the northernmost plateau of California. There, the cows roamed the foothills of Mount Shasta. An animal killed in the summer tasted markedly different from one killed in the winter. The latter thrived on the green grasses of California winter rains. The fat was different. You tasted the minerals. You tasted the land. You tasted the muscles. You tasted the beef. You tasted the age, how older beef compares to the commodity adolescent versions.

Grass-fed beef *looks* different, too. Most steaks in the butcher case look similar, regardless of the cow's diet, but when grass-fed subprimal cuts are divided into individual steaks during the butchery process, the meat flashes a fleeting, distinct green and blue hue in the moments before the blood oxidizes and turns the beef red. There's a vibrancy, a window into its provenance.

According to that aforementioned Stone Barns study, grass-fed beef is better for humans than its grain counterparts, with a "significantly better" omega-6 to omega-3 fatty acid ratio, higher levels of antioxidants, and a lower risk of *E. coli* infection and antibiotic-resistant bacteria.

Buying grass-fed beef is usually more expensive. I think the price is worth it, for the taste alone. Like any other food or drink—bread, gin, beer—it's the difference between an industrial product and one thoughtfully made by people. I would rather eat high quality beef less frequently than contribute to a broken system.

Let's Talk about Beef and Labeling

When buying beef, the burger maker has many options—grain-fed! grass-fed! pastured! grain-finished! plant-based! and on and on and on—so it's helpful to have a working understanding of what those terms mean.

All cows in America begin their lives eating grass. Most arrive at feedlots when they are around six months old, and from that point they are fed grain mixtures. These are grain-fed cows. Their feed is often laced with antibiotics because cows—ruminants whose digestive system is designed for a natural diet of pasture—are not built to easily digest grains, and so they cannot. As previously noted, their movement is minimal and thus that grain easily converts to fat. Usually, grain-fed beef has a greasier mouthfeel, with tasteless intramuscular fat. This meat has been engineered to be tender above all things. These cows are usually slaughtered in the ten-to-twelve-month range.

Grass-fed, grain-finished is a wholly useless and misleading term that is being increasingly used for marketing purposes. This can refer to nearly every single grain-fed cow.

The most common alternative to feedlots are cows that are grass-fed and/or pasture-raised. These terms are similar but not the same.

Grass-fed is exactly what it sounds like. According to the USDA, animals certified as grass-fed cannot ever be fed grain or grain by-products. Also, they must have continuous access to pasture during the growing season—that is, when they are putting on weight prior to slaughter—a definition that leaves room for cows to be kept in confinement (but still fed grass) for a portion of their lives. In terms of flavor, at its worst, grass-fed can taste watery and

full of minerals, especially iodine, with a lack of structure and lasting flavor; at its best, it is a pure expression of beefiness, terroir, and clean umami flavors. These creatures spend their entire lives in their natural environments, wandering sprawling hillsides and eating delicious grass all day, which results in stronger, more distinctive flavors. The beef generally contains less fat and is leaner. Most of these cows go to slaughter around the age of two years.

Pasture-raised refers to cows that spend their lives roaming pastures. But oftentimes, these cows may be given supplemental grain feed during winter months or even be finished on grain for the final weeks of their lives.

These are the basic definitions, but they're just that—basic. So much nuance goes into raising cattle, and the gray areas can be noble or more sinister. There are many ranchers who treat their cows with the utmost respect, and when the cow is ready to be slaughtered, gradually transition the feed from 10 percent grain to 90 percent grain over the course of months. Some smartly supplement with foraged grasses; some try to raise purely grass-fed cows in the wrong environments, so the cows become malnourished without a balanced diet. Others regularly feed corn and soy to their animals but still slap a "grass-fed" label on it. Still others have developed grass feedlots, which runs counter to the public notion of grazing animals.

As grass-fed beef has surged as a premium product, more and more ranchers hopped on the bandwagon. This has led to labeling shortcuts and deception, both made easier with a lack of industry enforcement.

Which beef should you buy? Grass-fed and organic. Ideally from a local ranch. The quick definition of organic beef is that the cows are fed only organic feed, and no hormones or antibiotics are used. Raising organic cattle in this fashion is more difficult and takes longer—and is thereby more expensive. I would encourage you to find an independent butcher who you like and trust, and take it from there. Ask your butcher about the meat, its provenance, and how it has been treated, both before and after slaughter. Definitely avoid frozen and prepackaged ground beef in general, and if dry-aged, grass-fed beef is available, try it. Find the beef you like.

The current beef ecosystem has been around for only the last half century or so. Immediately following World War II, American agriculture began to rapidly industrialize due to a convergence of factors. The increased availability of antibiotics allowed animals to be kept in close quarters indoors. Postwar mechanization left companies able to build factories and tractors in addition to ships and tanks. Advancements in biochemistry and petroleum-based fertilizer sparked monoculture crops like corn and soy, diminishing the productivity of the soils of the nation and threatening traditional regenerative farming practices. We tend to think of the rise of industrial farming as a gradual evolution, but in reality, it was a dramatic overhaul over the course of little more than a decade.

This is the system that Bill Niman faced when he began to rethink the beef game in California in 1969.

Cows and Beef and Burgers

The Story and Mission of Bill Niman

"Stop and listen," Bill Niman says, midstride, a half smile emerging as he looks out at his herd of cattle grazing on the grassy hills of Bolinas, California. Save for an occasional moan and groan from a particularly chatty calf, the field is mostly quiet, well isolated from the main roads, and especially from the bustle of Oakland, an hour southeast but a world away. "I love the sound of cows munching. You hear it?"

Faint waves crash in the distance, a reminder that Niman Ranch is perched high on sheer, steep cliffs overlooking foggy hidden beaches and the powerful Pacific Ocean. And once you notice that chorus of the cows eating the grass, you can't stop hearing it. It's a deep, almost crunching reverberation, the sound of these half-ton animals stripping leaves from wild plants. You feel the vibration of the deep roots, you smell the dry summer soil, and then you hear the sound of the cows—grass-fed cows—munching.

• • •

Niman Ranch is located on the literal edge of the continent, on a westernmost sliver of Bolinas, a small, unincorporated community in west Marin County, a short jaunt over the Golden Gate Bridge from San Francisco. Here, Bill Niman has managed to do something that so many of his contemporaries—food leaders and businesspeople alike—have failed to do: he changed the American food system in a real way.

Bill Niman has been here since the 1960s. For nearly all of those years, he has been raising animals on the land's rolling hills. He arrived as part of a convergence of like-minded people to the area, dreamers and idealists who left behind their city lives to get back to the land and live in a self-sufficient manner. In many ways, especially for Niman, such a move was a direct response to the industrialization of the food system. Gone were the idyllic family farms of his youth, the pigs and chickens he could see from the road while driving down the road in his native Minnesota.

> Niman Ranch is located on the literal edge of the continent, on a westernmost sliver of Bolinas, a small unincorporated community in west Marin County.

With this backdrop, the scene was set for the Bay Area to spark a new American food movement in the early 1970s. The California Certified Organic Farmers group was born in 1973, with the goal of defining organic standards and certifying organic growers. Within the greater Bay Area, west Marin found its niche as a small community of back-to-the-landers—people who wanted to feed themselves, their families, and their community. A few miles away from Niman's property, Warren Weber founded Star Route Farm in 1974. Not far away, there was Mark Pasternak's Devil's Gulch Ranch (1971) and the Zen Center's Green Gulch Farm (1972), among others. And, of course, Alice Waters's Chez Panisse, opened in 1971, was a platform for these farmers, its consumer-facing champion, its megaphone.

Niman's land was not—and still is not—particularly conducive for crops and horticulture. It's short on water supply and its growing season is limited. Throw in the consistent coastal breeze and a daily fog blanket, and it's not particularly well suited for much—that is, except for grass and cattle. (And, he likes to points out, maybe zucchini.)

He started with pigs and chickens, but cattle was where he made his name. You see, the ideal temperature for cattle is 57 degrees. And on his property, hugging the ocean, it's pretty much foggy and a glorious 57 degrees every single goddamn day. Happy cows with an ocean view, he likes to say. In those early days, he would feed his pigs spent barley from Anchor Brewing in San Francisco, the nation's first craft brewery, and old organic yogurt from Nancy's Yogurt, while eschewing the customs of animal production at the time—man-made compounds, antibiotics, growth hormones, and the like. "We just followed nature, if you will," he says with a matter-of-factness that belies the importance and, at the time, revolutionary nature of his actions.

When the rest of the world was moving pigs indoors, Niman kept them outside. He fed his cows the grasses of his hills, allowing them to convert indigestible plant matter into food that humans can eat—a symbiotic relationship of a most primitive manner.

"It was always, for me, important to represent the animals, the environment, and the farm community," Niman says. "Those are the three elements that conventional meat companies tend to torture in order to be profitable and drive costs down so they can compete."

"That's the antithesis of good animal husbandry, good farm community, and good environmental stewardship."

Pretty soon, he had a herd of cattle—acquired via some good old-fashioned bartering

involving tutoring—grazing on his fields, and like so many of his contemporaries, a lifestyle became a business. His land grew from the original eleven acres to the thousand it is today. Cattle roamed the hills, and Niman learned on the job, slowly but surely, getting guidance and mentorship from some neighbors but largely figuring it out on his own. And within a few years, he found himself listening to a new group of local folks: California's top chefs.

In the early 1980s, Niman began selling his meat to a natural foods grocery store in nearby Fairfax, and then a little more to another market a few towns over. Soon, chefs began calling. First came Chris Kump, son of James Beard Foundation founder Peter Kump, and Margaret Fox, a pioneer in the California cuisine wave, in some ways long forgotten in the twenty-first-century chef-loving Bay Area. At that time, though, she ran Café Beaujolais in Mendocino and was regarded in the same class as Alice Waters and Zuni Café's Judy Rodgers, both who also started buying his meat.

These early chef customers gave Niman feedback, told him how the beef was supposed to taste, what cuts they wanted. He listened, and adjusted.

Unlike the big cattle operations, his cattle were kept out on sprawling pastures for most of their lives, waiting 28 to 36 months—at least three springs—before being harvesting, about twice as long as the industry standard. In those early days, he was finishing his cows with grain, after raising them on grass. He avoided antibiotics, hormones, and many other mass-production practices that were standard at the

> **When the rest of the world was moving pigs indoors, Niman kept them outside. He fed his cows the grasses of his hills.**

Cows and Beef and Burgers

time. And, in another, very significant detour from his industrial counterparts, he was more concerned with expansion—both of his meat and his mission—than he was with profitability.

Above all, Niman was in the business of producing the Bay Area's best-tasting beef, and the business kept growing, adding one customer at a time, one farm at a time, building an empire anchored by that original Bolinas property and feedlot. Niman took care of his animals, his ranchers, and his customers. Niman Ranch meats soon found their way into Chipotle and Williams-Sonoma, and were the first carnivorous products at Trader Joe's.

Then, in 2006, he sold Niman Ranch.

. . .

This is where the story of Bill Niman gets interesting—but not for the reasons you might think. To this point, the Niman origin story is wonderful and fascinating, sure, but despite its incredible nooks and singular crannies it's not wholly original—in so much as Niman was part of a generation of ranchers and food producers who followed similar paths to culinary stardom; visionaries whose innovations redefined the industry standard.

What Niman was doing—raising animals humanely and naturally, without any man-made additives, in their natural environs—became mainstream. This is not to be understated. Today,

grass-fed beef is a quickly growing industry, doubling every year from 2012 to 2016, according to Nielsen data. It is so desirable that there are concerns about how the supply can appease the demand, and that's to say nothing of the murkiness of many grass-fed claims.

After Niman left the company he built, he started a new one: BN Ranch. This one would focus on beef that was solely grass-fed, differing from the early years when he raised the cows on pasture and eventually finished them on grain. He undertook the dual task of building a new company and proving that grass-fed beef could be every bit better than the alternative. He steadily built a new herd.

To help accomplish this, he opened his mind. He looked to other regions—and even other hemispheres. This is important, especially in the midst of a food movement that lionized local producers over everything else. Niman realized that when it comes to raising animals, sometimes local isn't always . . . better. If something is a state away, that doesn't automatically qualify it as not good, especially when that state might have the resources to do it better.

Just like cherries and nectarines, grass has a season. Here in California, the grasses at the foothills of the Sierra Nevada go to seed at different points in the year than the same kind of grasses in the Sacramento delta flatlands, for example. Grass isn't always in season, so grass-fed beef shouldn't either.

> **Niman was part of a generation of ranchers and food producers who followed similar paths to culinary stardom; visionaries whose innovations redefined the industry standard.**

Yet Niman saw ranches in California where animals were being raised in harsher environments, carelessly, and with less food, simply to quench a demand for *local* or *grass-fed*. Not only can such environments become more stressful for the animals, it's more resource-intensive for the rancher (and the planet). And shocker, undernourished beef doesn't taste as good.

So what did he do? He started looking elsewhere, because well, if you don't live in the right place, then maybe your cows would be better served if they were given some supplemental foraged grass during dry months, or perhaps they should be transported to grasslands. Or, if New Zealand is the absolute perfect place to grow grass-fed cattle, then maybe it's worth thinking about raising animals there, because if you want great grass-fed beef year-round, you may need to source from the southern hemisphere in our winter months, just like you would cherries or nectarines if you had to have them in December. Or, if you're in a place where both grass and forage are hard to find during the off-season, then maybe finishing grains are the best way to keep cattle in prime condition (just don't call that grass-fed beef).

It all depends so much on locale—altitude, latitude, proximity to the sea, rainfall. The lesson? There is no single best way. But you must follow nature.

Here's the thing about Niman: He is idealistic, but not dogmatic. So many of his contemporaries— his fellow pioneers and revolutionaries, if you will—were, and are, narrow-minded in their beliefs. Niman is not. He never stopped learning and listening. In those early years, he solicited advice from his neighbor ranchers and his chef buyers. Even now, nearly a half-century into his ranching life and a legend in his own right, he is still adjusting based on education and economics, be it a visit to Tasmania or a new study on beef ossification.

And throughout the decades, he has always kept an open mind.

For this reason, he became one of the few to transcend into the mainstream, serve good food at scale. That meant compromise at times, and staunchness at others. That meant an understanding that there is no single best way—for beef, for food, for life. In the process, he managed to do something: change the food system, in a real way. Not in a way that merely inspired or provoked, but in a way that got good food to the masses.

> **It all depends so much on locale—altitude, latitude, proximity to the sea, rainfall. The lesson? There is no single best way.**

Cows and Beef and Burgers

CREAM CO. AND THE CASE FOR EATING OLDER ANIMALS

Here is a brief story about a very good steer named Dogie.

Dogie was a larger-than-average, but nicer-than-most, cow who lived out on pasture on a ranch in Northern California. His days were spent puttering up and down the hills, chomping on grass, bellowing at the birds, and staring vacantly into the distance. He was so happy that he didn't even remember that he was castrated. One day, while wandering a far-off corner of one of his more favorite fields, Dogie returned to his herd and noticed that all his friends were gone. His brethren had all been picked up to go to slaughter, but he was left behind. His owner (Bill Niman) decided to keep him around.

Dogie lived to be a more-than-ten-year-old steer—and he grew to be a huge cow, a monster.

At long last, he caught the eye of José Andrés, a ground-breaking Spanish superchef with restaurants in D.C. and Vegas, among many other places. It was Cliff Pollard's job to get the cow from the field to the chef.

But there was a bit of a problem: The beast weighed over a ton, and for the life of him, or Dogie, Pollard couldn't find a slaughterhouse that could physically take it. He called every facility in California, and none had a heavy-duty enough rail system to hang it. The carcass would've literally broken the system.

Eventually, after much leg work and maybe a little sweet talking, Pollard found a slaughterhouse in Eureka that took the steer. Its hanging weight ended up being 1,300 pounds, which is about double the size of most commercial beef. He aged it for a few weeks, and went to Vegas for Andrés. The steaks that came off the steer were, as Pollard puts, "mind-blowing." It didn't even seem like beef; it was a completely different animal, almost like a wild version of itself. Even in its raw form, the meat was different; having been worked for a decade, the muscles were developed, clean, lean, almost floppy. The fat was thick and yellow. Once the meat was cooked, the differences completely emerged—its texture, its smell, the way it ate. It was crazy, funky, and unique.

The current standard age of cows used for conventional, industrial beef is in the ten- to twelve-month range; that's the age when the cows reach maturity, for the most part, which in turn means it's in the ranchers' best financial interests to send them to slaughter. The fewer resources dedicated to the animal, the higher the profitability. It is this cost/benefit comparison that has contributed in a large part to the current state of commercially raised animal. But older animals—six, eight, ten years old—possess a flavor profile that cannot be replicated in young cattle.

The act of older animal consumption has always been around, both in America and abroad—including in José Andrés's native Spain, where Galician cows produce some of the world's most prized beef and are killed when they are eight years old, at the youngest. The older an animal gets, the more flavor and nuance it develops, be it a lamb, a boar, or a cow.

The ten-year-old steer was more of a special-case scenario, but this is what Pollard does. He is the founder of Cream Co. Meats, a boutique meat distributor based in Oakland. He sells a variety of meats: heritage pork, pasture-raised lamb, chickens, and antique beef. In particular, Pollard has made a name selling older dairy cows.

Somewhere along the American cow industry's path—from its romantic cowboy roots to a big business that's ruled by faceless commercial interests—it split into two primary, and separate, realms: beef and dairy.

There's always been an open trade secret in the modern beef industry that old dairy beef goes to the Burger Kings and McDonald's of the world. They get the commodity version—the animals that have been culled from the herd because they can barely move, have been run into the ground, and have been sucked dry after a lifetime of being artificially propped up by hormones and antibiotics. When they finally stop producing milk, they are sent to the industrial slaughterhouse, many of which can process upward of 3,500 cows per day.

But there's another, smaller side to dairy beef, one with dairies that are more humane about their methods. These cows are not put to stress; they live on pasture their entire lives, and are milked twice a day, a world in which they are allowed to mature and develop flavor. This is more similar to preindustrialized days when a dairy cow would be used for its whole life, and when she was done, she would be slaughtered and turned into beef for eating. It is a system that makes sense in so many ways—not only does the cow live a full life, but it's also a more efficient, dual-purpose animal.

Instead of ending up in an industrial slaughterhouse that does thousands of cows a day, these cows land in an organic facility that processes about eighty per day. The reason for that huge number discrepancy? Organic cows, especially ones with age, come in all shapes and sizes, just like humans. Factory cows are bred, by design, to be the same shape and size for faster processing. *Meat shapes, not cows.*

California's Central Valley has always been a strong dairy region, and there are organic, pasture-raised cows that are being raised there. But until recently, those cows were largely relegated to the conventional market, so they were just grouped in with the factory farm cows—theirs was a shared fate of dog food and McWhoppers.

Pollard saw a new supply with some of the organic, pastured dairy cows. He worked with the ranchers to set standards for the meat of those animals and asked them to do something specific, in return for a higher payment than they would otherwise get. Among other requirements, he told them he was looking for large Holstein cows to be healthy, full figured, meaty, with a good fat cap. He paid them 15 to 30 percent more than the commodity market, slowly changing their minds about these animals' value and creating a new culture that gives them new incentives to keep the cows healthy.

At the slaughterhouse, seeing those cows next to the conventional ones is an amazing sight. The dairy cows—years older, fed on grass their entire life—look like dinosaurs next to their smaller brethren. Their skeletal structure is huge, their wingspan soaring.

The thing is, there simply aren't a lot of these animals, these organic, older, healthy dairy cows. Yet. The culture has not shifted so that the dairy farmers have enough incentive and education to eschew the conventional paths. And it's not only a beef thing; there's a finite supply of high-quality proteins in general. You can't just make more and more and more and more. Raising an animal the right way takes time.

Besides, the finances are a challenge. That ten-year-old steer that José Andrés got? If the true cost of that

> **But there's another, smaller side to dairy beef, one with dairies that are more humane about their methods.**

animal were to be passed on to the customer, then those would be some very, very expensive steaks (or burgers, or tartare).

For now, and the near future, dairy beef is, oddly, most likely to remain relegated to two extremes: the industrial and the boutique.

In America, beef gets graded on its quality. The top tier is Prime, which is described by the USDA as "young, well-fed beef cattle." The next two grades are Choice ("high quality, but has less marbling") and Select ("very uniform in quality and normally leaner than the higher grades"). After that, you've got Standard and Commercial, and then you get the bottom tier: Utility, Cutter, and Canner. Those are used for processed meats and dog food.

By USDA regulations, an animal cannot be graded Prime, Choice, or Select if it's older than thirty-six months, regardless of how idyllic its life was or how pristine its meat is. So who's going to want to serve Canner beef in a restaurant? Well, oddly enough, a lot of great chefs do. These days, Pollard and Cream Co. are usually sold out of their antique beef, which means that all the older dairy cows they are getting from the organic farms have already been claimed by local chefs.

> **For now, and the near future, dairy beef is, oddly, most likely to remain relegated to two extremes: the industrial and the boutique.**

Why are these cows so popular among the West Coast's top restaurants? It's not a marketing thing—if anything, the broader dining public generally has hesitation about a steak billed as "antique beef" or "old meat" or "a retired dairy cow who was going to become dog food but we, being self-righteous chefs, saved her."

No, the reason is simple: flavor. Beef from older cows tastes better than standard beef. It's so much more developed. It's more robust. It's sweeter. It just tastes *beefier*. Older versions of these products, like good ol' Dogie, have a completely different flavor—they're full of richness, nuance, maybe some funk, and loads of umami.

But, to be honest, older beef remains a challenge for most home cooks—let alone chefs—to purchase, even at a celebrated farmers' market or an upscale grocery store. I hope that changes in the coming years and decades. Perhaps, as seen in the grass-fed movement that blossomed into the mainstream in years past, the first step is raising awareness—among diners, among cooks, among restaurateurs.

At some point in the last several decades, the concept of "tenderness" somehow became the main rubric for determining the quality of meat, especially beef, and this shift came at the cost of flavor. Tender became the norm, the mantra for television advertisements and other beef-industry marketing. This benchmark was a false north, however, and one that encouraged killing animals earlier and earlier, and feeding them loads of fatty but flavorless grains. Finding value in certain nuances that have been lost in the country—like flavor—is a driving force behind eating older animals.

Flavor cannot be replicated in younger animals. Besides, there are other ways to achieve tenderness. Namely, dry-aging.

ON THE DISTINCT AND INIMITABLE GLORIES OF DRY-AGING

My love for dry-aged beef began with a hamburger. Two hamburgers, actually. First came the burger from Ryan Farr's 4505 Meats that was served at the Ferry Plaza Farmers Market in San Francisco; then came the Black Label Burger from Keith McNally's Minetta Tavern in New York City.

Both were revelations. I'm sure scores of hamburgers were made with scrap from dry-aged beef prior to these two, but I hadn't ever experienced one.

Eating the 4505 burger became my Thursday and Saturday farmers' market ritual. I would order them rare and eat them every week for breakfast. I would bring friends to try one, and I would go back for seconds. The burgers were the same size as the ubiquitous fast-food hamburger, but made with very high-quality, grass-fed beef from a Mendocino County rancher named Mac Magruder. And they were blessed with just enough dry-aged funk to propel them out of the realm of common hamburgerness.

This, combined with Swiss cheese and a rich butter-and-onion-heavy bun made for the best hamburger money could buy on the West Coast—all for seven dollars from a market stand.

That burger easily outclassed heftier, pricier, condiment-intensive versions from the best San Francisco restaurants.

On the other side of the country, Minetta Tavern was serving a burger that cost nearly thirty dollars. Made of dry-aged steak trim, it produced something unlike any meat sandwich I had eaten up to that point. It was the zenith of fine-dining hamburger, simple in its condiments, cooked to rare perfection, salty, and just big enough to satisfy without making you feel like you couldn't eat another, if push came to shove. That first Minetta Black Label Burger was as good as the steaks with which it shared space on the menu.

As the chef at Bar Tartine in San Francisco, I began to play with aging beef soon thereafter. I would buy some of the middle sections from 4505 Meats and age sirloin, rib-eye, and strip steaks. These experiments consisted of simply leaving the meat on the rack nearest the fan in the walk-in and allowing it to mature as long as possible.

Early trials of aging meat up to seventy days resulted in a couple of steaks that tasted like soy sauce and blue cheese—flavors I found interesting. Unfortunately, Chad Robertson and Liz Prueitt, Bar Tartine's owners, found those flavors offensive in the context of meat. We determined that thirty to forty-five days was the sweet spot for our rudimentary aging experiment, and left it at that.

A Traditional Method

There's a passage in Edna Lewis's seminal cookbook, *The Taste of Country Cooking*, where she describes a rural culinary ritual she undertook during the 1920s and 1930s. When winter arrived, her family would take a quarter of beef and hang it in the fresh air. Over the subsequent weeks, they would carve it piece by piece as they consumed it, slowly using the entire quarter throughout the icy season. A piece of fresh meat in December might be tight, lean, grassy, and chewy; in February, the cuts were likely looser, more tender and richer, and more full of umami.

The meat of older cows is much different than typical beef, regardless of its feed or environment. Yes, the meat tends to be richer and sweeter and more developed in flavor, but it can also be tougher and leaner. A fresh steak from an older working animal can be chewy. That's why, once upon a time, hanging it in the cold open air became standard practice—it turns tough meat into tender cuts. Visually, raw aged beef is a completely different color than its fresh counter-part; it's a dark ruby, almost brown color, versus the expected bright red.

Other folks, such as Harold McGee, have written better, smarter explanations on the scientific transformations that actually happen during the dry-aging process, but here's the basic version: When beef ages, its enzymes break down every molecule of the meat, turning (among other things) once-large pro-tein molecules into smaller, tastier protein molecules. This slow enzymatic breakdown greatly improves the flavor and texture of the meat. As Dr. Ali Bouzari writes in his book *Ingredient*, "Broken bits of protein make food tender and savory, bind water better, and brown faster." Those are all good things.

Dry-aging involves placing cuts of meat in a humidity- and temperature-controlled environment, result-ing in significant moisture loss. In other words, a 60-pound primal cut will turn into a 40-pound pri-mal cut; once it's trimmed and butchered, it will get even smaller. This is part of the reason why dry-aged beef costs more—there's waste.

When meat is placed in a dry-aging environment, a dry exterior quickly develops on the surface, creating a crust of sorts—think of how a whole loaf of bread gets stale around the edges first. The low tempera-tures and air flow limit the amount of mold that can develop. Over the course of the following weeks, the meat steadily loses moisture as the enzymes do their work and, as McGee describes in his book *On Food and Cooking*, that makes the meat more tender and the flavor more concentrated.

The meat loses moisture at a controlled rate and can age for months if desired, though roughly forty-five days is a sweet spot for burgers. When it's deemed ready to eat, any undesirable exterior pieces—such as any possible mold bits—are trimmed off, leaving behind a beautiful cut of beef that is incredibly different than the chunk of fresh meat that went in the refrigerator two months prior. Then, the whole cut goes through a grinder. The process is a continuation of bygone beef traditions, when humans would slaughter a cow only when it reached the end of its working life.

> **The meat loses moisture at a controlled rate and can age for months if desired, though roughly forty-five days is a sweet spot for burgers.**

Dry-aging definitely pro-duces better steaks. I think dry-aging makes a better burger. The meat dries nicely (and quickly) on its exterior, allowing the interior to stay juicy and rare. But as great as the texture is, it's the flavor that really sets dry-aging apart. Some eaters will say that they taste notes of dried fruit, blue cheese, nuts, grass, and malt, and they might be correct. But really, I don't think it's reductionist or an oversimplification to say that it just tastes more *like meat*.

Think of Parmigiano-Reggiano cheese, a Scotch whisky, a cured ham like prosciutto or jamón Serrano, or even a big red wine like a Cabernet Sauvignon or a Nebbiolo. Older versions of these products have a completely different flavor—they're full of richness, nuance, maybe some funk, and loads of umami. That concentrated flavor of beef—the essence of beefiness, if you will—is why dry-aged meat also works well in any application: Bolognese sauce, meat gravy (see page 128), tacos, meatballs, steaks, and, yes, burgers.

How to Dry-Age Beef (or Anything)

The most common way to age meat is a walk-in refrigerator with humidity control, but the basic properties are not too different from those old-time setups. There is a consistent airflow, and it's cold. It has a distinct smell; it's that same rich, nutty, sweet, almost fruity aroma of aged cheese or cured salumi.

At Kronnerburger, we use a mixture of cuts—aged on the bone—that come from grass-fed, pastured dairy animals that range in age from eight to twelve years old. The beef we age is slaughtered, hung for a day at the slaughterhouse, and then delivered to us the second day, and, crucially, without having been vacuum sealed, let alone frozen. (I have found that aged beef that has been vacuum sealed has a tendency to oxidize once it is ground; frozen beef, as noted on page 18, will produce shriveled patties.)

When it arrives, the fresh beef's weight and the date is recorded. Using a paper towel or clean rag, the exterior of the meat is patted as dry as possible, and then the meat is placed on racks in the dry-aging refrigerator. The first step in the process is to develop a dry exterior crust that acts a seal for the meat within. Constant airflow is crucial in developing this protective layer as quickly as possible, in about two days. The dry exterior allows for a controlled dehydration by providing a barrier against bacterial intrusion.

Once that coveted initial crust is formed, the beef is rotated 180 degrees. You want to dry the meat evenly. The meat should always be dry to the touch. It's important that the surface of the meat is as smooth as possible; cuts, folds, and gouges can create pockets of moisture that can cause spoilage. If any spoilage occurs, it should be cut out immediately. Maintaining as high a yield as possible, despite the loss of moisture, is crucial. If the beef isn't rotated or dried correctly and develops significant exterior mold, you increase the potential for "bad" mold, which in turn needs to get trimmed when grinding and thus means less dry-aged meat.

Speaking of which, a word about food safety. Sanitary conditions are very, very, very important while aging beef. Prior to aging, everything in the refrigerator—namely the racks—should be thoroughly sanitized, washed, and dried. The meat should never touch anything that hasn't been thoroughly sanitized, even for a second—this includes butcher blocks, scales, and such. If you need to remove the meat from the fridge, always keep a sterile environment: use plastic wrap on surfaces and plastic gloves if possible. During the aging process, the meat should never be slimy or have a strong odor; if you ever find a moist spot on the meat, flip it immediately so that the moist side is on top and thus exposed to open air. If you find a moist spot on the shelf or floor, wash the shelf immediately and thoroughly dry everything around it. Dry-aging, as the name implies, should be a clean and dry process.

Dry-Aging at Home

So you want to dry-age beef? It's a game changer and will result in a better tasting version of the beef you love. There is good news and better news.

The good news is that dry-aging beef is relatively easy and rewarding and delicious. You basically provide your current favorite piece of meat a cool and sanitary place to hang out with plenty of airflow. It sits in a meat locker for a month, and then it's more delicious than ever.

The better news is that doing it at home requires a widely available (and relatively cheap) piece of equipment. The easiest way to age beef, by far, is to use a dedicated refrigerator. At home, a small dorm room–style fridge works best.

Dry-aging beef has four basic necessities: refrigeration, controlled humidity, airflow, and, most important, time.

The process requires a fan that is powerful enough to constantly circulate large amounts of air through the space, producing perfect conditions to control the aging process. The sanitized racks that hold the meat should be food-grade plastic or metal wire racks, to allow airflow from all sides, especially the bottom. Ideal humidity is 80 percent, and the temperature is 40°F (4.4°C). While most refrigerators do not have humidity controls, we have found during our testing, a space as small as a minifridge maintains a relatively high level of humidity (perhaps thanks to the cooling element in the small freezer portion?).

Under these controlled conditions, you can age all kinds of beef from a minimum of thirty days all the way up to several months. Between thirty and forty-five days you should see a 20 to 30 percent reduction of water weight. The easiest way to track this change is by weighing your meat as you age it.

Remember those four basic dry-aging requirements? (Sorry for the pop quiz.) It's all about refrigeration, controlled humidity, airflow, and time.

Before we get into the best method, let's first hit the things to avoid. These are more accurately described as best practices, as opposed to cardinal rules.

- Don't use your everyday refrigerator. Unless you have a brand-new or completely empty refrigerator, the meat can pick up off smells from other items being stored—and vice versa. Dry-aged meat has a lot of exciting flavors, but "mélange of refrigerator inhabitants" should not be one of them.

- Do not age individual steaks. Given the moisture loss and potential need for trimming, it's just not practical to age an individual steak, especially for burgers. Primal or subprimal cuts are required for optimal dry-aging. The minimum weight is 10 pounds. A quick vocabulary rundown: The primal cuts are chuck, rib, loin, round, brisket, plate, and flank. Subprimal cuts are the size between primal cuts and portion cuts: the chuck roll, tri-tip, or top round.

- Don't wet-age. Wet-aging refers to the process of storing meat in Cryovac or plastic. You may get some enzymatic breakdown, maybe, but wet-aging is not an acceptable substitute for dry-aging. It's right there in the name, people. While it is a perfectly acceptable form of preservation, it does not in any way add to the flavor of the meat.

- Be clean. The meat must never touch any contaminated surfaces. This means everything it contacts must be sterilized: your hands, the rack, the fridge walls, the cutting board. This is important.

A recipe for dry-aging

1. Buy a dedicated refrigerator. To comfortably fit a fan on the floor and a large piece of meat or two on the racks above, you probably want a fridge that is at least three cubic feet. It provides space for a 10-pound chunk of beef on each rack, roughly 20 pounds total over two shelves—half a chuck and an eight-bone rib rack. (Side note: Some wine-storage refrigerators come with a humidity control and fans. Depending on the rack size and interior design, these are worth consideration.)

2. Once you have a fridge, buy a fan. Use a small electric fan with a long cord or an extension cord. The gasket on the refrigerator should close right over the cord, allowing the fan to be plugged in while the door is sealed. (Since the fan needs to be on 24 hours a day, avoid battery-powered fans, if possible; it will require replacing the batteries on an almost-daily basis, which is rather impractical.) And if you've gone this far, you might as well do it right. Buy a gauge that measures temperature and humidity; such devices are readily available online.

3. Run the refrigerator until cooled to the correct temperature.

4. Buy a piece of beef. A chuck cut into two (or four) pieces will provide enough meat for a few large burger parties. It will also allow you to age each piece for a different amount of time.

5. Once that coveted exterior dryness has formed (roughly after a day), flip the beef over. You want to dry the meat evenly. The meat should always be dry to the touch; it should not be sticky or slimy. If the conditions are right you should not see much mold develop. If mold does form, cut it off before using.

6. Try aging a piece for 14 days, another for 30 days, the third for 45 days, and the last for 60 days. The changes in texture and taste are significant and interesting. Find the amount of time that suits your dry-aged beef palate.

WHAT BEEF LOOKS LIKE AS IT AGES

FRESH

14 DAYS

30 + DAYS

Cows and Beef and Burgers

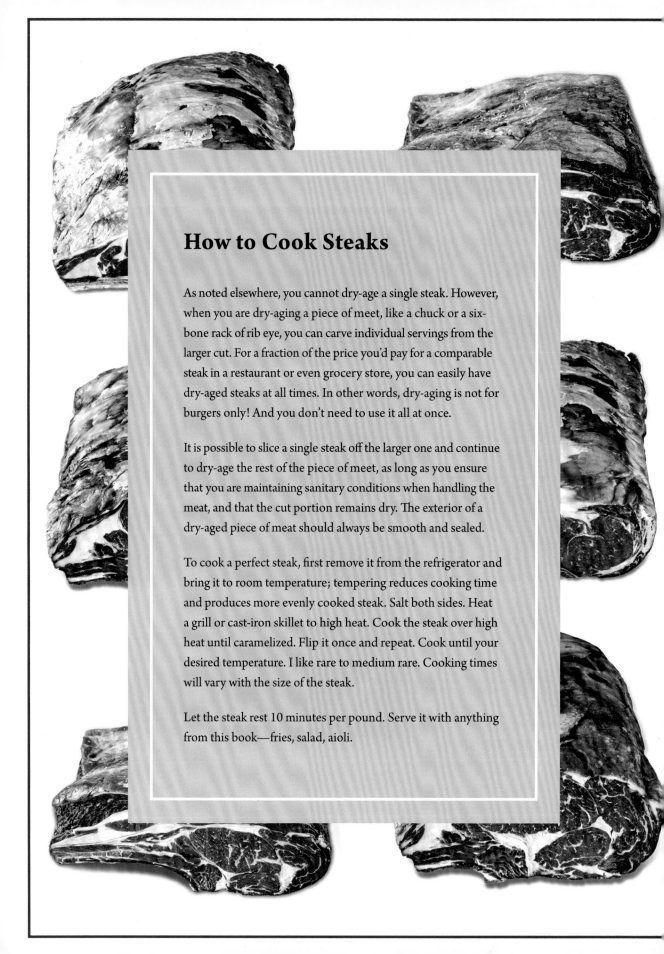

How to Cook Steaks

As noted elsewhere, you cannot dry-age a single steak. However, when you are dry-aging a piece of meet, like a chuck or a six-bone rack of rib eye, you can carve individual servings from the larger cut. For a fraction of the price you'd pay for a comparable steak in a restaurant or even grocery store, you can easily have dry-aged steaks at all times. In other words, dry-aging is not for burgers only! And you don't need to use it all at once.

It is possible to slice a single steak off the larger one and continue to dry-age the rest of the piece of meet, as long as you ensure that you are maintaining sanitary conditions when handling the meat, and that the cut portion remains dry. The exterior of a dry-aged piece of meat should always be smooth and sealed.

To cook a perfect steak, first remove it from the refrigerator and bring it to room temperature; tempering reduces cooking time and produces more evenly cooked steak. Salt both sides. Heat a grill or cast-iron skillet to high heat. Cook the steak over high heat until caramelized. Flip it once and repeat. Cook until your desired temperature. I like rare to medium rare. Cooking times will vary with the size of the steak.

Let the steak rest 10 minutes per pound. Serve it with anything from this book—fries, salad, aioli.

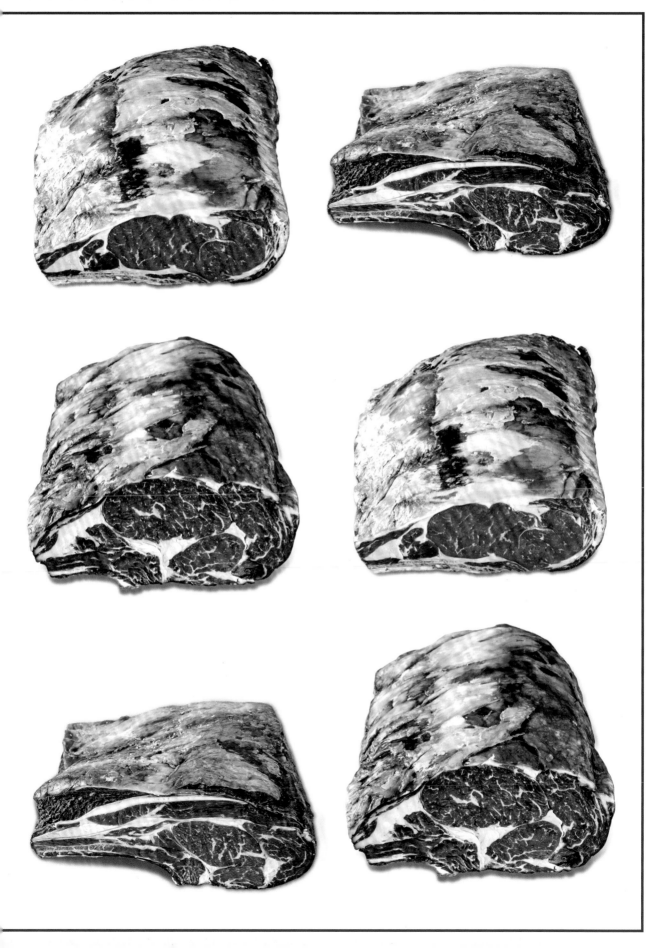

BETTER GRIND, BETTER BURGER

Freshly ground beef makes better burgers. Compare a burger made with prepackaged beef to one that has been freshly ground if you don't believe me. It is one of the simplest steps to improve the texture of the burgers you make.

I prefer a coarser grind. At the restaurant, we use a ³⁄₁₆-inch (4.5-mm; #32) grinder plate. With the Kronnerburger and most of my other burgers, I pass the meat through the grinder only once. Especially when dry-aged and cooked rare, the work that has gone into the treatment of the meat is best expressed with a coarse grind, very similar to a finely hand-cut beef tartare. (The one exception is the Otherburger, page 77, which I double-grind for a smoother, more unified, almost sausagelike texture.)

Grinding the beef yourself also allows you to control the ratio of lean meat to fat. A whole chuck should naturally consist of 15 to 20 percent fat. I buy fat to add to our grind to bring that percentage up to 30 percent. A butcher will have fat that can be added to the grind. A piece of brisket or short rib can also be used to add fat. Avoid waxy fat (like kidney fat); use firm fat that will cut, but not smear, when ground.

What should you look for when purchasing a grinder? The simple answer is power and sharpness. Metal grinder housings are preferable for the simple fact that they will get colder than their plastic counterparts. When grinding meat, the enemy is smeared meat. The function of a grinder is that it is cleanly cutting, not mashing, the meat into a paste. Cold grinders equal cold meat, which equal more precise cuts.

Just before grinding, cut the meat and fat into 1-inch chunks. Be sure to trim any mold that developed as a result of dry-aging; do not trim the fat.

Once the meat is cut, but before grinding it, chill everything in the freezer—that includes the meat cubes and all detachable grinder parts. Get the meat as firm as possible without being frozen, 15 to 25 minutes in the freezer; you want everything to be as cold as possible when you are grinding. Meat that is not kept cold while grinding will not cut as cleanly as correctly chilled meat.

The actual grinding process is straightforward, regardless of the type of grinder. Working carefully yet methodically, pass the meat through the grinder and then carefully put the ground meat on a plate or tray.

Portion the meat into loose balls, handling minimally. For Kronnerburgers (page 71), I divide the meat into 5-ounce rounds, which are slightly smaller than tennis balls.

Molding Patties

Using a ring mold is one of those simple tricks that will instantly improve your burger game. It creates burger patties of a consistent size, and hence consistent cooking time. It minimizes handling. It expedites the patty-making process, too.

Use a ring mold that is 4 inches wide and about 1 inch tall. Place the ring mold on a flat surface and cover it loosely with a small sheet of plastic wrap. Put a 5-ounce portion of meat on top of the plastic wrap and into the mold. Press down with the base of your palm, evenly distributing the meat within the mold. Use the plastic wrap to free the newly formed patty. Set the patty on a plate or baking sheet. Repeat as necessary.

If making a large number of burgers, stack the burgers with parchment or butcher's paper between the patties. Cover with plastic wrap and refrigerate until ready to cook.

Cows and Beef and Burgers

On Love and Rare Meats

By Harold McGee, author of *On Food and Cooking*

My father loved beef and lamb, and he loved them very rare.

That went for the hamburgers that he made during my Chicagoland childhood, seasoned with Lipton onion soup mix and grilled almost touching the charcoal. It also went for the hamburgers that he later enjoyed every Friday with his pal Harley Holt at Goldyburgers in Forest Park, where his standing order was a half-pounder waved for a few seconds in the general direction of the grill.

A few years after I came to the Bay Area, my father moved to a studio apartment in San Francisco, where he continued to indulge in super-rare burgers. But also began to suffer for them: several times he came down with various symptoms of food poisoning. When he told me about this he was around 80 years old. E. coli and salmonella and campylobacter can be life-threatening at any age, but the odds were especially unfavorable at his.

So I made a deal with him. If he would abstain from dodgy restaurant beef and make the hour-long trek to my place, then I would be his burger-waver. Every month or so I would buy a chuck roast, immerse it for a minute in a big pot of rolling-boiling water to pasteurize its surface, grind it, salt it and form it lightly, and grill the patties the way he did back in the day. He never got sick from burgers again. And I don't think he missed the soup mix.

COOK BURGERS ANYWHERE

(Also, Salt Your Burgers!)

I have cooked burgers everywhere, and I have served burgers to loyal customers everywhere: in a dark nightclub, in a dead-end alley behind a coffee roastery, on the sidewalk. You, too, can cook burgers anywhere. All you need is fire and a grill—no machines, no special culinary techniques. Cooking burgers is elemental—a piece of meat put next to the heat of a fire.

Don't have a barbecue setup? Make your own box from bricks or cinder blocks and put a grill grate over it.

Salt

One of the most crucial steps in burger-making is burger-salting. I recommend a coarse kosher salt, such as Diamond. Once your patty is formed, right before cooking, sprinkle each side with ½ teaspoon of salt, using a total of 1 teaspoon of salt per burger. This makes all the difference in the world. Salt your burgers.

Fire

There is no equivalent to the flavor imparted to burgers—or anything, to be honest—by a wood-burning fire.

At Kronnerburger, I cook in what is essentially a hearth: three walls made of bricks that refract the heat, with a steel grate whose height is adjusted using a crank. I build a fire against the back wall and as the wood turns to coal, I pull it forward beneath the cooking surface and add fuel to the fire at the back of the hearth.

We use the fire to prepare much more than the burgers. We often grill or char vegetables for salads and side dishes, we toast bread, and we use the smoke from the fire to flavor everything from cured fish to coconut milk (see page 163). Building a fire and cooking with it has become a very important part of my restaurant. If you have the space for a large wood grill or even a Weber from the hardware store, there is so much that can be done with a wood fire.

When using a Weber or a grill in a park, I build a fire that fills the entire vessel. Once the wood has burned to coals, I feed fresh wood into the fire on one side and use the opposite side to cook. It is essentially the same setup as the hearth in the restaurant—just smaller. I have even cooked for large groups using two Webers, one to keep a constant fire to draw coals from, and the other to actually cook over.

Grill burgers over coals, as opposed to open flames. Your coals should be glowing and hot, but the wood beneath your burgers should not be aflame; sporadic flames are fine, but you don't want a raging fire. When your coals are hottest, the grill grate should be about 6 inches above the heat. If you don't have robust coals, you can position the grill grate about an inch above them.

If you're using a gas grill, do not cook over high heat, as it will create flare-ups and uneven cooking. Instead, preheat the grill on high heat for at least 5 minutes, and then when you're ready to cook, turn it down to medium.

Rare

The Kronnerburger uses freshly ground dry-aged beef, which is best when cooked rare, with a charred exterior and warm but still dark-red interior. Over a hot fire or ripping-hot flat surface (like a griddle or skillet), the burger needs only 3 minutes of cooking time: 2 minutes on the first side, a flip, and then 1 minute more. For unaged beef, many people may prefer their burger medium-rare, 1 to 2 minutes more on the second flip.

A fire, from its inception
to the point when it's
ready to cook burgers.

On Fire

By Lee Desrosiers, chef of Achilles Heel in Brooklyn, New York

I stare into the fire and I forget that I am in one of the largest cities in the world.

Not long ago, this part of northernmost Brooklyn, just off the East River, looked like a corner that New York had completely forgotten. In the early 1900s, dock workers would frequent this place, but these days, new construction threatens to swallow it up.

Here, in a fire cage made of bricks, metal pipes, and chain link, set in a parking space behind the bar, is where I enjoy freedom. We call it "wild" West Street, because it feels like anything goes. Exposed to the elements, we hang lamb legs above smoky logs, bury vegetables in hot ashes, and slowly smoke fish nailed to boards. Every Sunday morning, we build three fires and hang guinea hens above the grill table to smoke. Later, they get pressed into cast iron Dutch ovens, buried in ashes and coals to steam, and after a long rest in their juices, grilled once again over piping hot embers fresh from the fire. Schmaltz collects on the ashes and stains the bricks.

I stare into the fire and I forget about the buildings and the machines and I focus on the food. No timer is set, no temperature is measured. All that matters is what you observe, what you smell, and what you feel. And the results of this journey are among the most delicious things.

KRONNERBURGER

KRONNERBURGER

KRONNERBURGER

CHAPTER TWO

KRONNERBURGER

KRONNERBURGER

KRONNERBURGER

KRONNERBURGER

KRONNERBURGER

KRONNERBURGER

KRONNERBURGER

KRO

KRO

KRO

KRO

KRO

KRO

KRO

KRO

KRONNERBURGER

KRONNERBURGER

KRONNERBURGER

KRONNERBURGER

KRONNERBURGER

KRONNERBURGER

KRONNERBURGER

KRONNERBURGER

THE

ERBURGER

ERBURGER

CHAPTER TWO
THE KRONNERBURGER

KRONNERBURGER

KRONNERBURGER

KRONNERBURGER

THIS IS THE KRONNERBURGER

The Kronnerburger is the culmination of many hamburgers eaten and many more cooked, of open pasture and fire, of years and months and weeks of experimentation and research and failures, of modernism and classicism, and, most of all, of thoughtful reductive simplicity. A distillation of every failure and every success.

The actual Kronnerburger burger patty takes 3 minutes to cook: 2 minutes on one side, 1 on the other. To get to those final 180 seconds requires patience. Patience that starts with a cow, and a lot of grass. Our cow spends 8 to 12 years eating grass and making milk, producing food daily. Once the cow is harvested and butchered, it spends an additional 30 to 60 days dry-aging, slowly but surely becoming more tender and concentrating all of the flavor derived from a long life of healthy grazing. When Hamburger Day finally does arrive, the beef is coarsely ground and cooked over the hot coals of an oak fire. For a mere 3 minutes.

The result of this beautiful, arduous odyssey is a perfect patty: charred and crisp on the outside, juicy and pink on the inside, full of savory intensity. Maybe you care deeply about the journey; maybe you don't care about anything. I just hope you can be patient and enjoy the burger.

You see, the Kronnerburger itself is just a hamburger, but each component is thoughtfully considered. The beef is the star, and the entire process leading up to the climax — cow, grass, time, fire—is designed to maximize that idea.

This is a burger constructed to put the beef on a pedestal. That also means that the noise of most burgers is stripped away. No bacon, no melted cheddar cheese. (Note: we make other burgers that have lots of cheese and bacon; see chapter 3.) The modern "restaurant chef who doesn't actually want to serve a burger burger" has taken a turn toward the maximalist, layering novelty toppings atop novelty toppings, with gold leaf, meat "jams," doughnuts, foie gras, ramen noodles, pineapple, horseshoe crabs, laserdiscs, and so on. The Kronnerburger looks toward familiarity, simplicity, and function. What's adding crunch? What's adding creaminess? What's adding something? And most of all, what highlights the beef?

You spent all this time and effort aging, grinding, cooking, and maybe even reading about your beef. Doesn't it make sense to serve a burger that showcases that work?

Burger Station

When cooking (or grilling), burgers come together quickly.
Most patties, from rare to well-done, cook in a matter of
minutes. As such, it's very important—essential, even—to
have all your ingredients prepped before starting, so you
can build and then eat your burger(s) in a timely manner.

Your burger station should have all the condiments at the
ready. Lettuce cleaned and separated into leaves. Tomatoes
sliced. Onions charred. Pickles, pickled. Mayo ready to
be spread.

Ideally, your buns should toast while the burgers cook—
you want both to be finished at roughly the same time.
This may prove tricky at first, so you may want to employ
a friend, spouse, or eager child to be in charge of toasting
buns. Safely involving a child is especially helpful in creating
burger inclusiveness. In terms of timing, err on the side of
toasting your buns first and then finishing the patty.

PAIN DE MIE BUN
(AKA OFFICIAL KRONNERBURGER BUN)

The burger bun must be soft and pliant, always toasted, yet textured enough to corral everything between its two hemispheres. The bread should be sweet, moist, and light, but not so fatty as to make the burger unnecessarily greasy.

The burger bun should add a certain amount of its own taste and texture, but should not be too assertive an element. It is utilitarian. It should soak up meat juices, but not crumble in your hands. It should be referential to childhood burgers, a vehicle for deliciousness, and simultaneously strong enough to maintain the structure of the whole, yet pliable enough to avoid attracting too much attention.

To avoid overly bready burgers, the burger buns should be the exact same diameter as the patty—4 inches for the Kronnerburger—and only 50 percent taller. These buns are about 1½ inches tall, compared with the uncooked patty's 1-inch height.

Prior to opening, we tested the burger buns over and over, tweaking the flour percentages a sliver this way and another tiny amount that way. This is where we landed.

4 cups plus 2 tablespoons (518 grams) all-purpose flour

3 tablespoons plus 1 teaspoon (33 grams) potato flour

3 tablespoons (35 grams) sugar

¼ cup (27 grams) milk powder

1 tablespoon plus 1¼ teaspoons (12 grams) kosher salt plus another pinch for the egg wash

1 tablespoon plus 1½ teaspoons (18 grams) active dry yeast

2 tablespoons (15 grams) nutritional yeast

1½ cups (361 grams) water, plus another ¼ cup for an egg wash

4 tablespoons (55 grams) unsalted butter, at room temperature, cut into teaspoon-size pieces

1 egg

MAKES 12 BUNS

Line a baking sheet with greased parchment paper.

Into a stand mixer fitted with a dough hook, add the all-purpose flour, potato flour, sugar, milk powder, salt, dry yeast, and nutritional yeast and mix briefly to combine.

With the mixer on low speed, add the 1¼ cups cold water and butter and mix for 7 minutes, until well incorporated. Increase the speed to medium and mix for another 7 minutes.

Transfer to a covered container and allow to rest, refrigerated, for 12 hours. (Note: this stage is optional, but recommended.)

Remove from the refrigerator. Divide the dough into twelve portions, each the size of a large plum or about 2½ ounces (75 grams).

Working with one piece of dough at a time on a lightly floured work surface, roll the dough into balls.

Connect your thumb and index finger and form a cage—your thumb and the edge of your pinkie should be the boundaries—and use the base of your hand and your fingers to roll the dough into a taut ball. Put on the prepared baking sheet and let rise until doubled in size, about an hour.

Using your palm, flatten the balls gently into 4-inch rounds; let rest for another 30 minutes.

While you wait, preheat the oven to 450°F and make an egg wash. Stir together the egg, the remaining ¼ cup water, and the remaining pinch of salt in a small bowl. When the buns have rested for 30 minutes, use a pastry brush or paper towel to lightly brush the buns with the egg wash.

While the oven heats to temperature, fill one or two oven-safe containers—cast-iron pans work great—with ice or water and place on the bottom rack of the oven. The goal here is to create a steamy environment in the oven to ensure a nice, crusty outer layer on the buns. Let steam for 10 minutes. When the oven reaches temperature, refill the pans with water and at the same time, put in the buns on the top rack. Bake for 12 minutes, until golden brown. Let cool before slicing for burgers.

Save extra buns for future burger fun and freeze up to a month.

Note: For the bread and pastry recipes in this book, measurements are often given with weight and volume. This is for accuracy's sake, because weight measurements are so much more exact than volume. Also, if you're going through the trouble of making your own buns, it's worth it to invest in a scale—digital ones start at just over ten dollars.

How to Buy Buns

Congratulations to you if you want to bake buns for your burger. If you don't have access to pain de mie or (not-too-fatty) brioche buns, the best alternative is white bread buns.

Yes, *those* buns. You may not have realized it—or maybe never appreciated it—but those are serviceable buns. Those buns that come eight to a pack, automatically packaged in a clear plastic bag. Those buns that come either with or without sesame seeds. Those buns that you remember from special meals in your grandmother's backyard. Those buns that are admittedly flavorless.

Yet the great revelation that those buns spark is that the main function of a burger bun is mechanical support. Buns are vehicles. Buns are not the stars of the burger show. So if you don't have access to a great-tasting and freshly baked bun, you can make the best of that soft white guy found in every grocery and corner store.

White bread buns—and to a lesser degree, potato rolls—are soft and spongy, yet strong and pliant enough. In a finished burger, the halved bun gives way between your fingers, flattening ever so slightly and molding to your grip. Whether toasted or not, the bread keeps its integrity through the entire eating process, affording evenly distributed bites of all the burger components.

Other bun choices do not share these qualities. Crusty ciabatta loaves and hard French rolls are too bready and firm, and the meat and lettuce will run off when you bite into a burger made with either option. No good! Mass-produced brioche rolls will crumble in the face of a juicy burger and its condiments, leaving you with burger debris to be salvaged with your greasy fingers. You know the feeling.

DILL PICKLES

Salt, acid, texture. The dill pickle, heavy on aromatic spices, is an essential foil to the richness of the burger. This recipe should yield about a quart of sliced pickles, enough for at least ten burgers, but they will keep indefinitely in the refrigerator. For all your pickle needs.

1½ pounds pickling cucumbers

2 tablespoons kosher salt

2 tablespoons dill weed

1 small white onion, quartered through the root end

2 cloves garlic

2 tablespoons coriander seeds

1 tablespoon plus 1 teaspoon caraway seeds

1 tablespoon dill seeds

1 tablespoon black peppercorns

2 teaspoons mustard seeds

1½ teaspoons anise seeds, or 1 star anise pod

1 teaspoon fennel seeds

½ teaspoon celery seeds

4 whole cloves

4 allspice berries

2 bay leaves

2 cups distilled white vinegar

MAKES 1 QUART

Wash the cucumbers well. Trim off and discard the ends, then cut the cucumbers into ¼-inch slices. Put the cucumbers in a 1-quart sealable plastic container or mason jar. Add the salt and dill weed and toss to evenly distribute.

Heat a pot over medium heat. Add the onion, garlic, coriander seeds, caraway seeds, dill seeds, black peppercorns, mustard seeds, anise seeds, fennel seeds, celery seeds, cloves, allspice, and bay leaves and toast the spices until fragrant, about 1 minute.

Toss the spices often during toasting to be sure they don't burn. Add the vinegar, turn the heat to high, and bring to a simmer. Once the vinegar mixture reaches a simmer, remove from the heat and let cool for 5 minutes.

Prepare an ice bath that will fit the base of the pickle container.

Take a foot-long square of cheesecloth and drape it over the top of the pickle container to create a strainer. Pour the hot vinegar mixture, including the spices, onion, and garlic, through the cheesecloth and into the container with the cucumbers. The cheesecloth should catch the solid ingredients. Twist the corners of the cheesecloth together to turn it into a spice-filled bundle that will sit in the brine atop the cucumbers. You want the spices to be in the brine but not among the cucumbers. If necessary, tie the cheesecloth bundle up with kitchen twine.

Make sure the cucumbers are completely submerged in the brine by shaking the container and stirring the contents if necessary.

Put the container—with the spice bundle—in the ice bath and let cool. Once cooled, eat immediately or store indefinitely in the refrigerator. The spice bundle can be left in the container for up to 1 week.

CHARRED ONION

There are many schools of thoughts surrounding onion on a burger. Some prefer raw. Some like grilled. I like to split the difference, and so I slice it and cook just one side. This allows the best of both worlds: you get the smoky char of grilled onions but still maintain the spicy crunch of raw onions. The charred side also adds a bit of smokiness to burgers that are cooked indoors in a pan.

These can be cooked in advance, or around the same time as the burgers.

1 red onion, cut into ⅓-inch slices, making sure to keep the rings intact

MAKES ENOUGH FOR 4 BURGERS

To cook on a grill: Place the onion slices over direct heat. Keeping the onion rings in slabs, as opposed to individually separated, makes for easier handling. Let them be about 1 minute over the fire, unmoved, until charred on one side.

To cook on a stove top: Heat a cast-iron skillet over high heat. When it's ripping hot, put the rings on the skillet and cook for 2 to 3 minutes, unmoved, until charred on one side.

Remove from the heat and let cool before serving.

CHEDDAR MAYONNAISE

The cheddar mayonnaise hits the richness of mayo and the spicy, acidic flavor profile of mustard, with the textural benefits of both. It references the sauciness of melted American cheese, but with a lot more flavor and no chemical stabilizers. Also, turning the cheese into a mayonnaise is fun.

6 egg yolks
2 tablespoons distilled white vinegar
1½ teaspoons mustard powder
1½ teaspoons kosher salt
2 cups neutral oil (such as safflower oil)
6 ounces aged sharp white cheddar
(such as Welsh cheddar, New York cheddar, or Spring Hill Jersey cheddar), grated

MAKES 3 CUPS; ENOUGH FOR 15 TO 20 BURGERS

Add the egg yolks, vinegar, mustard powder, and salt to a food processor and process until combined, about 30 seconds. The volume should increase by about half.

With the processor running, very slowly pour in the oil, almost at a drip, and then gradually increase the speed of the pour. If the oil starts to build up on the surface of the sauce, slow down the pour. The mixture will slowly thicken and ripples will form, as the mayonnaise's texture gradually builds.

When you've added all the oil, add the cheese and process until completely smooth. Store for 1 to 2 weeks in the refrigerator. Serve cold.

ROASTED BONE MARROW

When it comes to the Kronnerburger, bone marrow is a condiment, not a side. When thinking about reductionism and simple ingredients, what is more elemental to pair with any piece of beef—be it a steak or burger—than bone marrow, the essence of a cow? Use liberally.

4 (3-inch) marrow bones, halved lengthwise
2 tablespoons red wine vinegar
1 tablespoon kosher salt
Flaky sea salt

MAKES ENOUGH FOR 4 BURGERS

Put the marrow bones in a sealable container, preferably a jar or plastic quart container. Add the vinegar and kosher salt and enough water to cover. Cover and refrigerate for 24 hours.

Just before cooking the burger, preheat the broiler. Remove the marrow bones from the brine and place on a baking sheet. Broil until the marrow is cooked but not yet rendered and still solid, about 7 minutes. Sprinkle with flaky sea salt. Keep warm until serving.

TOMATO

When in season, there is nothing better than a perfect slice of ripe tomato. If you're using a larger heirloom variety, one big slice, the same diameter as the patty (4 inches), should suffice for a single burger. If you're using smaller tomatoes, like Early Girls perhaps, you'll need three to four slices to cover the burger.

1 medium-large tomato

MAKES ENOUGH FOR 4 BURGERS

Remove the stem and slice off the top of the tomato. Place the tomato on its side. Slice vertically into ¼-inch-thick slices; discard top and bottom portions. Set slices aside on a plate until the burger is ready to assemble.

LETTUCE

Lettuce provides the crunch, the crispy, the cool. But the lettuce component should not overwhelm. A couple of leaves will suffice. Make sure to discard any watery ribs.

1 head of iceberg lettuce

MAKES ENOUGH FOR 4 BURGERS

Remove the core and any ugly exterior leaves. Separate remaining leaves from their ribs. Rinse under cold water and dry. When ready to serve, tear the leaves into patty-size pieces, so they do not have a chance to escape the hemisphere of the bun. Expect to allocate 3 to 4 small leaves per burger.

KRONNERBURGER:
A BURGER TO BELIEVE IN

1½ pounds dry-aged, grass-fed chuck

4 Pain de Mie Buns (page 62 or store-bought)

2 tablespoons unsalted butter, at room temperature, plus more if using a stove top to cook the burgers

4 teaspoons kosher salt (1 teaspoon per burger; ½ teaspoon per side)

12 to 16 dill pickles slices (page 64; 3 to 4 per burger)

Charred Onion (page 65)

4 to 8 slices tomato (if in season; 1 to 2 per burger)

12 to 16 torn iceberg lettuce leaves (3 to 4 per burger)

¼ cup Cheddar Mayonnaise (page 65; 1 tablespoon per burger)

Roasted Bone Marrow (page 66, optional; 1 bone per burger)

SERVES 4

Cube the meat and chill on a tray in a freezer until firm but not frozen, 10 to 15 minutes. Following the grinding instructions on page 47, coarsely grind the meat.

Divide the beef into four 5-ounce balls, handling minimally. Put a sheet of plastic wrap over a 4-inch ring mold on a cutting board or other hard surface. Put a ball in the middle of the mold and gently press down with the palm of your hand, forming a patty that is 4 inches wide. Pop it out with the plastic wrap. Put the patties on a large dish or small baking sheet and refrigerate until ready to cook.

Before you begin cooking the burgers, get the buns toasting. Heat a cast-iron skillet or similar surface over medium-low heat. Slice the buns in half horizontally. Smear the butter on the buns and place, butter side down, on the hot surface, working in batches if necessary. Toast until golden brown, 6 to 8 minutes, adjusting the heat if necessary. You want to do your best to time their completion to the burger cooking.

While the buns toast, cook the patties. Salt both sides of each patty, using about ½ teaspoon for each side, meaning about 1 teaspoon total per patty.

To cook on a grill: Cook the patties over direct heat (but not roaring flames) for 2 minutes, then flip and cook for another 1 minute, until cooked rare.

To cook on a stove top: Heat a skillet over high heat. Smear butter on one side of the patties (this helps with caramelization) and cook for 2 minutes. Flip and cook for another 1 minute, until rare.

Place a patty on a bottom bun and cover the patty with three to four pickle slices. Top with one or two rings of charred onions, one or two slices of tomato, and three to four good leaves of lettuce. Spread 1 tablespoon of cheddar mayonnaise on the top bun and cap it off. Repeat with your other burgers. Serve alongside the bone marrow, allowing eaters to apply the marrow as they wish. Eat immediately.

CHAPTER 3

OTHER BUR
OTHER BU
OTHER
O

OTHER BURGERS

PATTY MELT

Behold the most comforting recipe in the book, a holy union of burger, cheese, and a hot skillet. Where the namesake Kronnerburger is restrained and contained, the patty melt is its messy opposite. It is the maximalist answer to the Kronnerburger's minimalism.

Traditionally, the patty melt is a simple griddled sandwich of sliced buttery rye bread, beef, caramelized onions, and a melted cheese of some sort, usually Swiss. As with many of the recipes in this book, this version takes those tenets and reconsiders each one. The onions are cooked in beef tallow to infuse extra flavor, and sharp cheddar is a more vibrant option than Swiss. A touch of rich béchamel lends creaminess, so Chinese hot mustard is essential to balance out the equation.

Be mindful of how thickly you slice your bread; as with standard burgers, you want an optimal bread-to-meat ratio, so keep the bread thickness roughly equivalent to the burger patty thickness—a little over a half-inch.

Patty melts are the best. Crunchy, chewy, spicy, and cheesy—all of the things at once. Long live the patty melt, an indulgent chunk of Americana that will thrust you back to an era of diners that have long since disappeared.

CARAMELIZED ONIONS

5 tablespoons rendered beef tallow or unsalted butter

1 white onion, thinly sliced

Kosher salt

PATTY MELT

1 pound freshly ground dry-aged, grass-fed beef

5 tablespoons unsalted butter, at room temperature

8 slices levain (page 231 or store-bought)

¼ cup Chinese hot mustard

¾ cup grated sharp cheddar cheese

2 tablespoons kosher salt

¼ cup béchamel

SERVES 4

To make the onions: Melt the tallow or butter in a frying pan over medium heat. Add the onion, turn the heat to medium-low, and cook, stirring occasionally, until golden brown, 30 to 45 minutes. Season with salt. Remove the onion from the pan and set aside until ready to serve.

To make the patty melt: Preheat the broiler.

Divide the beef into four 4-ounce balls, handling minimally. Put a sheet of plastic wrap over a 4-inch ring mold on a cutting board or other hard surface. Put a ball in the middle of the mold and gently press down with the palm of your hand, forming a patty that is 4 inches wide. Pop it out with the plastic wrap. Put the patties on a large dish or small baking sheet and refrigerate until ready to cook.

CONTINUED

Using 4 tablespoons of the butter, butter one side of each of the levain slices and place, buttered side down, on a baking sheet. Spread the mustard on the unbuttered sides of four of the slices and top the other four slices with the cheese. Put the baking sheet under the broiler until the cheese melts and begins to get a touch of color, 4 to 5 minutes. Remove from the broiler.

While the bread toasts, cook the patties. Heat a skillet over high heat. Salt both sides of each patty with ¼ teaspoon salt and put them on the hot skillet. Cook until deeply browned on one side, about 2 minutes, then flip the patties and cook until they're a nice medium-rare, another minute or so.

Put a patty on a slice of bread with cheese and top with caramelized onions. Spread 1 tablespoon of béchamel on a mustard bread slice and cap the sandwich. Repeat with your other sandwiches.

Heat the remaining 1 tablespoon butter in the same skillet over medium-high heat. Retoast the sandwiches in the skillet, one or two at a time, until crisp, about 1½ minutes on each side. Keep warm while the others cook. Slice in half and eat immediately.

BÉCHAMEL

- 1 tablespoon unsalted butter
- 1 tablespoon all-purpose flour
- ¾ cup milk
- ¼ cup heavy cream
- 1 bay leaf
- Dash of red wine vinegar
- 1 pinch of kosher salt
- 1 pinch of freshly ground black pepper
- 1 pinch of ground nutmeg

MAKES ABOUT 1 CUP

Melt the butter in a small saucepan over medium heat. Whisk in the flour and cook, whisking continuously, until golden brown, 6 to 7 minutes. Whisk in the milk and cream and add the bay leaf. Keep whisking and cook until the béchamel boils and starts to thicken, 4 to 5 minutes. Remove the pan from the heat and stir in the vinegar, salt, pepper, and nutmeg. Remove the bay leaf. Pour into a bowl to cool. Can be stored, covered and refrigerated, up to 3 days.

OTHERBURGER
(SERVED NOT RARE)

Front and center on the restaurant's menu is our signature burger, which from day one has been billed thusly: "Kronnerburger (served rare)."

Served rare. It's hard for me to admit, but even with superwonderful beef, a rare burger is not for everyone. However, when it comes to grass-fed beef—especially grass-fed beef that's dry-aged and coarsely ground—longer cooking time yields diminishing returns. The more aged beef cooks, the drier and more texturally unpleasant it becomes, even more so than conventional beef. So what's a burger cook to do if some folks want a well-done burger? A cook's got to give the people what they want.

Which brings me to the Otherburger, a Kronnerburger alternative that is served *not* rare.

If you're grinding your own hamburger meat, take note, because there are two things that enable a burger to be juicy *and* well-done. First, the blend should be 30 percent dry-aged beef, 30 percent fresh (that is, non-aged) beef, and 40 percent beef fat. The finishing touch? A double-grind— putting the meat through the grinder twice, making for a smooth texture. If you're a more casual burger-maker who perhaps does not grind your own meat, this is still a fine burger to make— just use the fattiest ground beef blend you can get.

Above all, the Otherburger is a direct descendant of the fast-food burger, the genre popularized by the likes of In-N-Out. The patty is thin and griddled, and the accompaniments are straightforward, vintage Americana: shredded iceberg lettuce, American cheese, and an Othersauce that bears a striking resemblance to Russian dressing. This is a burger that's rooted in nostalgia and cooked beyond rare.

CONTINUED

Other Burgers

OTHERSAUCE

3 tablespoons Cheddar Mayonnaise (page 65) or store-bought mayonnaise

2 tablespoons ketchup

1 tablespoon diced dill pickles (page 64 or store-bought)

1 teaspoon mustard powder

BURGER

10 ounces grass-fed chuck (preferably 5 ounces dry-aged, 5 ounces fresh)

6 ounces raw beef fat

½ red onion, cut into slivers

2 tablespoons unsalted butter, at room temperature, plus another 2 teaspoons for cooking the burger

4 Pain de Mie Buns (page 62 or store-bought)

Kosher salt

4 slices American cheese (page 221 or store-bought)

1 cup shredded iceberg lettuce

4 thin slices tomato (when in season)

SERVES 4

To make the Othersauce: Combine the mayonnaise, ketchup, pickles, and mustard powder in a small bowl and mix well. Set aside until ready to serve.

To make the burger: Cut the chuck into 1-inch cubes. Be sure to trim any mold that developed as a result of dry-aging; do not trim the fat. Chill everything—that includes the beef cubes, the beef fat, and all detachable grinder parts—in the freezer until the beef is firm to the touch. Mix the meat and fat together in a bowl. Using the same grinder plate as the standard Kronnerburger (page 47), pass the mixture through the grinder twice.

Divide the ground beef into four equal balls. With the beef lost to the grinder, each of the patties should weigh about 4 ounces. Put a ball on a cutting board or other hard surface and gently press down with the palm of your hand, forming a patty that is 4¾ inches wide. Put the patties on a large dish or small baking sheet and refrigerate until eating time.

When ready to cook, preheat the broiler.

Soak the red onion slivers in ice water for 10 minutes. Drain and let dry on a paper towel.

Before you begin cooking the burgers, get the buns toasting. Heat a cast-iron skillet or similar surface over medium-low heat. Slice the buns in half horizontally. Smear the 2 tablespoons of butter on the buns and place, butter side down, on the hot surface, working in batches if necessary. Toast until golden brown, 3 to 4 minutes, adjusting the heat if necessary. You want to do your best to time their completion to the burger cooking.

While the buns toast, cook the patties. Heat a second ovenproof skillet over high heat. Salt both sides of each patty, smear ½ teaspoon of butter on one side of the patties and put them on the hot skillet. Cook until caramelized, about 3 minutes, then flip the patties, lay the cheese on top, and put the skillet under the broiler until the cheese melts, 1 to 2 minutes.

Spread 2 teaspoons of Othersauce on the bottom bun and add the lettuce, tomato, and onion. Add the burger patty. Spread 2 teaspoons of Othersauce on the top bun and cap it off. Repeat with your other burgers. Eat immediately.

Why Burgers?

The topic of burgers is a window into everything that is beautiful and horrible about America. Burgers *are* America. As American as road trips or blue jeans or jazz. Nearly everyone has eaten a burger and has some nostalgic fondness for it. Burgers exist in infinite variations in every part of this country and have reflected the zeitgeist for more than one hundred years. From a democratic square meal in a Depression-era town to the height of indulgent excess in a neon-filled Vegas casino, the hamburger embodies America in all its complexity.

Stop at an In-N-Out Burger on California's Interstate 5 and look at the parking lot; you'll see electric cars parked next to heavy-duty pickup trucks, and every variation of American silently sharing in the equalizing experience of the roadside hamburger.

But the burger illuminates the darker side of our country, too. Can America—in all of its fire-breathing awesomeness—continue to exist as our resource-intensive way of life nears an end? Can we eat so much meat per year, if the cost of that consumption is destroying our farmland, air, and water? And can we do that if it's also making us sick? Like it or not, we cannot.

If you look a little more closely at the treatment of industrial feedlot animals, the lives of the farmworkers who tend to them, and the toll the sad feedlots take on our shared environment, those 99-cent fast-food hamburgers aren't such a value.

You may have heard all of this information before but still feel like your seemingly small decision to buy a burger can't effect positive change on a large scale, which is not entirely true. It turns out, you don't need to buy a Prius or punch a dolphin hunter to take a stand, although the latter would be a very noble action.

You can make a statement through your food choices, your purchases, your money. And because the burger is so ubiquitous and so tied to America's nostalgia for its collective food memory, it is uniquely positioned as a near universal way to making more thoughtful, conscientious decisions about how we feed our families and how we define our planet's future—it's an entry point.

That's why burgers.

EARTH BURGER

The goal of the Earth Burger is simple: To create something that is as satisfying as meat, without the meat. The misstep of most vegetarian or vegan burgers, in my opinion, is that they are trying to replicate meat instead of making something that is delicious on its own merit. From a technical standpoint, a veggie burger also needs to have the right texture and maintain its shape while being eaten.

The journey to arrive at the Earth Burger recipe was rather arduous: patties made with beets, patties made with dried fava beans, patties made with garbanzos, and patties made with just about every conceivable tofu concoction. The usual veggie burger foundation of grains or beans seemed too expected. Nothing tasted quite right or had the right character. And if it did, it didn't hold together during cooking and eating. Frying the patty twice was a revelation on the texture side, but there was still something missing. (If you are newbie to the technique of frying at home, feel free to skip ahead to page 123 for a quick lesson.)

Then we turned to mushrooms. After many trials and experiments, we settled on this recipe— a mushroom-heavy, umami bomb of vegetables and tofu, bound by potatoes and potato starch. The mushrooms come in both roasted and powder forms; the latter is available at Asian markets and online, and is an easy way to add loads of savoriness, almost like salt on steroids. The combination worked, and I've continued to refine it through the years. It's vegan and gluten-free, too.

And the name? It materialized when we were half-seriously brainstorming the most self-righteous, crunchy name we could possibly come up with. It stuck.

1 pound brown mushrooms, coarsely chopped

4 ounces carrot, coarsely chopped

4 ounces broccoli, coarsely chopped

4 ounces cauliflower, coarsely chopped

4 ounces green cabbage, coarsely chopped

12 ounces firm tofu, drained and cut into small dice

1 large sweet potato, unpeeled

1 Yukon gold potato, unpeeled

5 tablespoons potato starch

2 teaspoons mushroom powder

1 teaspoon kosher salt

2 teaspoons liquid aminos

1 teaspoon sherry vinegar

4 cups rice bran oil or other neutral oil

4 Vegan Buns (page 226 or store-bought)

2 tablespoons unsalted butter (or oil, if vegan)

4 squares Yuba Bacon (page 220, optional)

Charred Onion (page 65)

4 to 8 slices tomato (if in season; 1 to 2 per burger)

10 to 12 iceberg lettuce leaves

12 to 16 dill pickle slices (page 64 or store-bought)

¼ cup Tofu Mayo (page 218) or regular mayo

SERVES 4

CONTINUED

EARTH BURGER, CONTINUED

Preheat the oven to 400°F. Line one roasting pan or sheet pan with parchment paper.

Put the mushrooms, carrot, broccoli, cauliflower, and cabbage in the prepared pan. Put the tofu in a small baking dish or on a baking sheet. Wrap the sweet potato and potato in aluminum foil. Put everything in the oven.

Roast the tofu until browned, about 15 minutes. Set aside. Roast the vegetables until lightly browned and caramelized, about 30 minutes. The doneness will vary among the different vegetables, but that's okay, because it will add to the texture of the final product. Let cool slightly. Shred the roasted vegetables in a food processor or meat grinder; if you have neither, chop the vegetables as finely as possible. Roast the potatoes until very soft, 50 to 60 minutes. To check for doneness, gently remove the potatoes from the foil—they should be very soft when touched. Let cool slightly.

Using a stand mixer fitted with the paddle attachment, mix the potatoes and their peels with the potato starch, starting on low speed and gradually increasing the speed until the texture is gummy and glutinous, about 1 minute. Set aside.

In a large bowl, stir together the finely chopped vegetables and the potato mixture. Add the cooked tofu, the mushroom powder, salt, liquid aminos, and sherry vinegar. Stir gently to combine; the mixture should feel similar to the texture of raw ground beef. Divide the mixture into four equal balls.

Put a sheet of plastic wrap over a 4-inch ring mold on a cutting board or other hard surface. Put a ball in the middle of the mold and gently press down with the palm of your hand, forming a patty that is 4 inches wide. Pop it out with the plastic wrap. Put the patties on a large dish or small baking sheet.

Now it's time to fry the Earth Burgers at a low temperature; this initial fry is not meant to fully cook the patty, but ensures that it retains its shape during the final cooking. In a Dutch oven or heavy pot, heat the oil to 340°F over high heat. Working in batches, fry the burgers until cooked through, about 3 minutes. Adjust the heat as needed to maintain the oil temperature at 320°F. Using a spider skimmer or other small strainer, remove the burgers from the oil and drain on paper towels. Let cool. Put the patties on a large dish or small baking sheet, cover with plastic wrap, and freeze until firm, at least 1 hour, or up to 4 days.

When ready to serve, get the buns toasting. Heat a cast-iron skillet or similar surface over low heat. Slice the buns in half horizontally. Smear the butter (or oil, if you're going vegan) on the buns and place, butter side down, on the hot surface, working in batches if necessary. Let slowly toast until the burgers are done. The buns should develop a nice golden brown.

Heat the same oil (or the same amount of oil) to 395°F over high heat. Fry the burgers a second time until brown and crispy, 3 to 4 minutes. Adjust the heat as needed to maintain the oil temperature at 375°F. Remove the burgers from the oil and drain on paper towels.

Place a patty on a bottom bun and top with the yuba bacon, onion, tomato, lettuce, and pickles. Spread 1 tablespoon of tofu mayo on the top bun and cap it off. Repeat with your other burgers. Eat immediately.

Note: The patties are best made ahead of time. Fry them the first time and then they can be frozen in a sealed container for up to 4 days.

BREAKFAST BURGER

The Breakfast Burger is a quite malleable recipe. Neither the types of patty nor bun really matters—use beef or pork; a biscuit or sliced white bread. Try it with an Earth Burger and an English muffin. Or perhaps a Pork Burger and a pita pocket. The world is full of opportunity.

Really, it is more of an idea than a burger. The idea, as it were, is to put an egg on anything, add any further toppings you might have in your fridge to quench your morning needs, and thereby dub it a breakfast burger. Not only is it a great way to start your morning, but you'll quickly learn that it can also put you back to sleep. It is the ideal sandwich to bookend your slumber.

EGG CUSTARD "PATTIES"

8 eggs

¼ cup crème fraîche or sour cream

2 ounces cream cheese, at room temperature

1 pinch of kosher salt

BURGER

4 to 8 strips bacon

20 ounces freshly ground dry-aged grass-fed beef, or other meat of your choice

Kosher salt

4 tablespoons unsalted butter, at room temperature

4 biscuits (page 230), split

4 to 8 tablespoons Pimento Cheese (page 135) or other desired cheese

A few handfuls of dill pickles (page 64, or store-bought) on the side, for serving

SERVES 4

To make the egg custard "patties": Preheat the oven to 300°F.

In a large bowl, stir together the eggs, crème fraîche, cream cheese, and salt until thoroughly combined. Pour into an 8-inch square baking dish, smooth the top, and cover very tightly with aluminum foil, making sure it's airtight to enable steaming. Bake until the custard sets, about 35 minutes for a jiggly custard; or longer if you prefer your custard to be firmer. Remove the foil and plastic and let cool. Cut into four equal square patties.

To make the burger: Meanwhile, heat a skillet over medium heat. Working in batches, if necessary, cook the bacon to your desired doneness.

Divide the beef into four 5-ounce balls, handling minimally. Put a sheet of plastic wrap over a 4-inch ring mold on a cutting board or other hard surface. Put a ball in the middle of the mold and gently press down with the palm of your hand, forming a patty that is 4 inches wide. Pop it out with the plastic wrap. Put the patties on a large dish or small baking sheet and refrigerate until ready to cook.

Salt both sides of each patty, using about ½ teaspoon for each side, meaning about 1 teaspoon total per patty.

Heat a skillet over high heat. Smear the butter on one side of the patty (this helps with caramelization) and cook for 2 minutes. Flip and cook for another 1 minute, until rare.

Place a meat patty on a split biscuit and top with an egg custard "patty," some cheese, bacon, and pickles. Repeat with your other burgers. Eat immediately and enjoy the rest of your day.

CRAB BURGER

In the Bay Area, making good use of Dungeness crab is a must. The original incarnation of the Crab Burger more closely resembled a fish sausage or fish cake, with a smoother, more processed texture. We've since worked our way back to something that is more closely aligned with a crab cake, which is less bready and a truer representation of the crab.

The secret ingredient that ties it all together is rockfish. Rockfish is a light and flaky white fish that just so happens to be a top option for sustainability on the West Coast, especially the California coast. In the Crab Burger, rockfish helps round out the texture, differentiating it from a bread-heavy crab cake. The resulting patty falls somewhere between a crab cake and a Filet-O-Fish. Plus, given that a pound of Dungeness crab meat can cost up to forty dollars, blending in rockfish has an economic benefit as well.

You can either deep fry the patty (see page 90) or cook it in a skillet; the former will result in a crispier and juicier final product. If you fry the patties, I recommended chilling them in the freezer until firm, and then frying.

7 Pain de Mie Buns (page 62 or store-bought)

8 ounces raw rockfish or cod fillet, minced

1 egg, lightly beaten

Zest of 1 lemon, plus lemon wedges, for serving

1 tablespoon freshly squeezed lemon juice

1 tablespoon chopped fresh flat-leaf parsley

2 teaspoons fish sauce

2 pinches of kosher salt

8 ounces cooked Dungeness crab lump meat (see page 90)

2 tablespoons unsalted butter at room temperature, plus 1 teaspoon for cooking the patties

1 tablespoon neutral oil (such as safflower oil)

12 to 16 ribbons Pickled Carrots (recipe follows)

¼ white onion, thinly sliced

1 small watermelon radish, cut into matchsticks

1 head Little Gem lettuce, separated into leaves

Leaves from 1 bunch cilantro

¼ cup tartar sauce (page 220 or store-bought)

SERVES 4

Preheat the oven to 350°F.

Put three of the buns in a food processor and process until they reach a fine, almost sandy texture. Set aside. Remove a third of the crumbs—about 1 cup—and reserve for later. Spread the remaining crumbs on a rimmed baking sheet and bake until dry and crunchy, 10 to 15 minutes. Set a timer so you don't burn them.

In a large bowl, combine the toasted bun crumbs, untoasted bun crumbs, rockfish, egg, lemon zest, lemon juice, parsley, fish sauce, and salt and, using your hands, mix well. Gently incorporate the crab.

Chill in the freezer until firm, about 30 minutes.

Divide the crab mixture into four balls. Put a sheet of plastic wrap over a 4-inch ring mold on a cutting board or other hard surface. Put a ball in the middle of the mold and gently press down with the palm of your hand, forming a patty that is 4 inches wide.

Pop it out with the plastic wrap. Put the patties on a large dish or small baking sheet, cover with plastic wrap, and freeze until firm, 30 minutes.

Before you begin cooking the burgers, get the buns toasting. Slice the buns in half horizontally. Heat a cast-iron skillet or similar surface over medium-low heat. Smear the 2 tablespoons butter on the remaining four buns and place, butter side down, on the hot surface, working in batches if necessary. Toast until golden brown, 6 to 8 minutes, adjusting the heat if necessary. You want to do your best to time their completion to the burger cooking.

While the buns slowly toast, cook the patties. Heat the oil and remaining 1 teaspoon butter in a skillet over high heat. Add the frozen patties and cook until golden brown, about 4 minutes on each side.

Place some pickled carrots, onion, and radish on a bottom bun. Top with the patty, followed by the lettuce and cilantro. Spread 1 tablespoon tartar sauce on the top bun and cap it off. Serve immediately with lemon wedges.

PICKLED CARROTS

1 large carrot, peeled
2 cups rice vinegar
1 teaspoon coriander seeds
1 teaspoon sugar
1 teaspoon kosher salt

MAKES ABOUT ½ CUP

Using a mandoline or vegetable peeler, thinly shave the carrot lengthwise. Put the carrot ribbons in a sealable jar or plastic container.

Combine the vinegar, coriander seeds, sugar, and salt in a small saucepan and bring to a simmer over medium-high heat. Simmer for 5 minutes, and then pour the hot vinegar mixture over the carrot and let cool. The pickles are ready to eat when cool. Cover and store indefinitely in the refrigerator.

FRIED CRAB BURGER

4 Crab Burger patties (see page 88)

2 cups fine rice flour

2 tablespoons potato starch

2 tablespoons cornstarch

1 teaspoon paprika

Kosher salt

¾ cup sparkling water

4 cups rice bran oil or other neutral oil, for frying

2 tablespoons unsalted butter, at room temperature

1 cup shredded lettuce

4 Pain de Mie Buns (page 62 or store-bought)

¼ cup tartar sauce (page 220 or store-bought)

SERVES 4

Make sure the crab burgers are firm and chilled, which helps maintain their shape when cooked.

In a large bowl, stir together the rice flour, potato starch, cornstarch, paprika, and a pinch of salt. Transfer ½ cup of the rice flour mixture to a second bowl. This second bowl is your dry dredge. Add the sparkling water to the large bowl, whisking until smooth; it should be saucy enough to coat the back of a spoon. This is your wet dredge.

In a Dutch oven or heavy pot, heat the oil over high heat to 385°F, making sure you have 2 inches of oil. Working with one patty at a time, dip the frozen crab patties into the dry dredge bowl, evenly coating them, and then dip into the wet dredge. The liquid should coat the patty, but not be heavy or gloppy. When the oil hits 385°F, fry the patties until golden brown, about 8 minutes, working in batches if needed to make sure the patties don't touch each other. Adjust the heat to maintain the oil temperature at 365°F. Using a spider skimmer or other small strainer, remove the patties from the oil and let drain on paper towels. Sprinkle with salt as desired.

While the burgers fry, get the buns toasting. Heat a cast-iron skillet or similar surface over high heat. Slice the buns in half horizontally. Smear the butter on the buns and place, butter side down, on the hot surface, working in batches if necessary. Toast until golden brown, 2 to 3 minutes, adjusting the heat if necessary. You want to do your best to time their completion to the burger cooking.

Place some lettuce on a bottom bun and top with a patty. Spread 1 tablespoon of tartar sauce on the top bun and cap it off. Repeat with your other burgers. Eat immediately.

How to Cook a Crab

Depending on the size of the crustacean and the dexterity of your hands, one Dungeness crab will yield about 8 to 16 ounces of meat. A general, if sweeping, rule of thumb is that the crab meat yield will be a quarter of the original crab's weight.

Cooking a Dungeness crab is simple. To cook a live crab, bring a large pot of water to a boil. Salt it generously. Working one at a time, drop the crab in the boiling water for 15 minutes, then remove. Cool by placing under cold running water.

To clean it, first remove the abdomen, the small triangular flap of shell on the underside of the crab. Then remove the large top shell by grabbing the ledge right above the eyes and pulling upward. Under cold running water, remove the sponge-like gills and mandibles. Break the crab in half along the natural divide in the crab's body. Extract the meat from the body. Using your hands or a crab cracker, extract the meat from the claws and legs. Refrigerate, covered, and use within 24 hours.

On California, Burgers, and Democratic Dining

When I first arrived in California around 2001, I was introduced to Chad Robertson, the owner of Tartine Bakery. Chad would become my friend and sometime employer. Together, we would often go the Slow Club, a now-closed restaurant in San Francisco (see page 94), after work or before seeing live music. Chad would bring Tartine loaves for Sante Salvoni, who was the chef there at the time, and we would share burgers and pasta.

Where the original hamburger was invented seems to be a point of contention—I'm sure there's a more scholarly book that can better explain its origin story—but I do believe the modern burger came into its own in California.

The hamburger has long played a prominent role in California's pop culture. Long before it spawned McDonald's and Jack in the Box outposts across the country, Southern California gave us the perfect paper-wrapped burgers of the Apple Pan, the greasy gut-bombs of Bob's Big Boy, and the ground sirloin "hamburger de luxe" of the Brown Derby.

Southern California is where the burger became a part of American culture. It's where the drive-in was popularized and where the drive-through became a late-night staple. The burger was an essential player in the diner alongside milkshakes and fries, almost like an extra in films such as *American Graffiti* and *Pulp Fiction*, where "this is a tasty burger" was immortalized.

Burgers are inseperable with American culture.

The burger joint was a fixture in the Bay Area, too, and a rundown of the bygone burgers of the bay is a history lesson in landmark restaurants. Kwik Way in Oakland had that Jetsons look, a 1950s vision of the space age, with its green-neon sign lighting up the entire block. Elsewhere in Oakland, JJ's featured a Frisco Sourdough Burger.

Doggie Diner and Mel's carried the torch for the archetypal midcentury diners in San Francisco, alongside other haunts like the Hippo on Van Ness and Blum's, the latter where you could get those burger-sundae combos (or as one newspaper clipping put it: "a fair shake and a better burger"). And nothing says old San Francisco more than Red's Java House, a time capsule literally sitting on the dock of the bay, where you feel the past not only through the ghosts of the longshoremen that used to fill up the little waterfront shack, but through its burger, a remnant itself—a crusty sourdough roll stuffed with a thin burger patty, bright yellow mustard, chopped white onions, and, if you're lucky, a pickle slice or two. Get it with a bottle of Budweiser and some soggy fries for a few extra bucks; that's the combo meal.

Specialty burgers were signatures at Original Joe's and Joe's of Westlake (charbroiled burgers, to be precise) and Balboa Café (the proto bar burger). At Joe's Cable Car in the Excelsior, Joe Obegi bragged that he would grind his beef daily. The burger made inroads into fancier places, too. Vanessi's on Broadway served a "perfect pink burger," not far from another late-night burger joint, Clown Alley, famously greasy and slightly terrifying if clowns aren't your thing.

The burgers at these relic establishments are firmly planted in time, and almost certainly embellished with the rose-colored glasses of nostalgia. But here's the thing: they were all beloved. Burger tales are thick around this region, especially among old-timers, or, at least, newspaper archives. And most had one thing in common—fair, accessible prices.

When it comes to restaurants, burgers are democratic. They are everyday restaurant food and have played this role in America for decades. Even during the Depression, people saddled up at lunch counters across the country for slugburgers or dirtyburgers—flat, skinny burgers made with a little bit of precious beef that was stretched further with soy or other ingredients. From the Dust Bowl to drive-ins, from sock hop–swinging teenagers and longshoremen to late-night drunks and eccentric filmmakers, the burger played the same role: a democratic meal.

That indelible quality would prove to be essential to the next evolution of the burger: the restaurant burger.

The late '80s and early '90s were a watershed moment for the burger genre, as more and more fancy chefs started playing with it, bringing it into the fine-dining realm. Southern California may have staked its claim in burger pop culture with the fast-food burger, but it was San Francisco and the Bay Area that opened a new chapter.

At Zuni Café, home of famous chickens and perfect salads, Judy Rodgers offered a burger only during lunch and late-night services. The grass-fed meat was—and still is—salted the night before, coarsely ground the day of, sprinkled with salt and pepper, and cooked. It is served on a slab of grilled rosemary focaccia with pickled onions, aioli, and, when in season, tomato slices. A few blocks away were Hayes Street Grill and the bygone Stars, where Patricia Unterman and Jeremiah Tower, respectively, served thoughtful burgers for operagoers, alongside trail-blazing California cuisine with impeccably sourced seafood and produce. The burger suddenly had gravitas, a legitimacy that came from its place on the city's best menus.

> **From the Dust Bowl to drive-ins, from sock hop–swinging teenagers and longshoremen to late-night drunks and eccentric filmmakers, the burger played the same role: a democratic meal.**

Closer to downtown, Bix had a truffle burger, and Boulevard had a special Wagyu beef lunch burger. A decade or so later, Nopa opened on Divisadero and rolled out its beefy burger, a whopper (pun only slightly intended) of a grass-fed patty, cooked over wood and served simply on a brioche bun. Soon, a burger on a mid- to upscale restaurant menu would become the norm, rather than the exception.

A burger on a menu at a place like Zuni or Bix was—and still is—a blessing for those who are not looking to drop an entire paycheck on dinner. More often than not, the burger is the cheapest entrée, and it's usually half the price of its cohorts, the steaks or fish fillets. And it comes with added value like fries, onion rings, or a side salad. A burger is a back door into a fancy restaurant.

Somewhere in the middle of all that, I found myself in San Francisco, living on a young cook's salary.

The quandary of being a young person in the restaurant industry is that you are infatuated with food and eating. This is an interest that most often leads to fancy restaurants, a problem for a young cook with no money. A burger was a reasonable entry point into San Francisco fine dining for a cook making $9.75 per hour, and the Slow Club's was my favorite.

A burger on a menu was an oasis. And so I would go to the Slow Club. I would go by myself, sometimes with a friend. I would wrangle a seat at the bar and order a burger.

SLOW CLUB BURGER

I knew the Slow Club first as a customer, and then as a cook, and eventually as the chef. Opened in 1991 in a once-industrial corner of San Francisco, the Slow Club was one of those extraordinary, atypical restaurants that set out to be a simple neighborhood restaurant, but ended up being consequential.

It helped define a part of the city at a very specific time, tucked between the eastern reaches of the Mission and the western edge of Potrero Hill. It brought a minimalist, spare aesthetic to casual restaurant design. It was cool, dark, and comfortable. It survived twenty-four years of dot-com boom and bust and boom and bust, until finally closing in 2015.

Most important, it served an excellent burger.

The Slow Club burger was made with beef from Bill Niman (see page 28). The patty was on the larger side—6 ounces—and cooked to a perfect medium-rare. It was served on a grilled bun with balsamic onions, mustard, aioli, and a handful of mesclun.

After working for a year and a half at my first cook job in San Francisco, I found myself as the massively underqualified sous chef of the Slow Club. Sante Salvoni was the chef, and we had a serious love-hate relationship with the Slow Club burger. We ate them before or after (and sometimes before *and* after) work nearly every day and served around eighty of them a night, all off an 18-inch grill that also was the cooking surface for two other entrées.

Sante's food was excellent across the board, but every night it seemed like every other dish that left that tiny kitchen was a burger. We offered the burger with cheddar, Jack, Swiss, or Gorgonzola. This created endless opportunities for modification, making the conversations between kitchen and server wonderfully annoying. Server: "What do you mean you won't put three kinds of cheese on one burger and cut it into three cheese-specific triangles?" Sante: "Fuck you."

It also led to some delicious off-menu burger creations, mostly involving blue cheese. Sante would stuff blue cheese *in* burgers for his friends, making for a dressed-up Jucy Lucy. And then there was the Jesse Koide special. Jesse, another cook there, would make a burger topped with blue cheese, and then cover it in enough plastic wrap to protect it from nearly any act of God and stick it in his bag. By the end of the night, it would congeal into a uniform beef-and-blue-cheese mess.

The Slow Club burger sent me down my path of burger fanaticism. This recipe is also the ideal burger that's made from supermarket ingredients. If you like cheese and a medium-rare patty made with readily available grass-fed beef, this is your burger.

CONTINUED

SLOW CLUB BURGER, CONTINUED

BALSAMIC ONIONS

1 tablespoon neutral oil (such as safflower oil)

1 red onion, thinly sliced

Kosher salt

⅓ cup balsamic vinegar

BURGER

1½ pounds freshly ground grass-fed beef (preferably chuck from BN Ranch)

4 sturdy, non-brioche burger buns or Pain de Mie Buns (page 62 or store-bought)

2 tablespoons unsalted butter, at room temperature, plus another 2 teaspoons if using a stove top to cook the burgers

Salt and freshly ground black pepper

4 slices of your favorite cheese (such as Swiss, Jack, or cheddar), or 4 ounces blue cheese

4 to 8 slices tomato (if in season; 1 to 2 per burger)

4 handfuls of mesclun mix

¼ cup aioli (page 219) mixed with ¼ teaspoon freshly ground black pepper

SERVES 4

To make the onions: Heat the oil in a saucepan over medium-high heat. Add the onion and cook, stirring occasionally so it doesn't scorch, about 5 minutes. Once the onion has some color, add a generous pinch of salt, stir, and cook for 5 minutes more. Stir in the vinegar, turn the heat to low, cover, and cook until the vinegar is slightly reduced and the onion is glazed, 8 to 10 minutes. You want the onion to maintain some texture—not turn into soup. Remove from the heat and set aside until ready to serve.

To make the burger: Divide the beef into four 6-ounce balls, handling minimally. Put a sheet of plastic wrap over a 4-inch ring mold on a cutting board or other hard surface. Put a ball in the middle of the mold and gently press down with the palm of your hand, forming a patty that is 4 inches wide. Pop it out with the plastic wrap. Put the patties on a large dish or small baking sheet and refrigerate until ready to cook.

Before you begin cooking the burgers, get the buns toasting. Heat a cast-iron skillet or similar surface over medium-low heat. Slice the buns in half horizontally. Smear the 2 tablespoons of butter on the buns and place, butter side down, on the hot surface, working in batches if necessary. Toast until golden brown, 6 to 8 minutes, adjusting the heat if necessary. You want to do your best to time their completion to the burger cooking.

While the buns toast, cook the patties. Generously salt and pepper both sides of each patty.

To cook on a grill: Cook the patties over direct heat for 3 minutes, then flip, add the cheese, and cook for another 3 minutes, until medium-rare (or longer, if desired).

To cook on a stove top: Heat a large cast-iron pan over high heat. Spread ½ teaspoon of butter on the bottom of each patty. Add the patties and cook on one side for 4 minutes, then flip, add the cheese, and cook for another 2 minutes, until medium-rare.

Place a heaping forkful of balsamic onions on a bottom bun and top with a patty, tomato, and some mesclun. Spread 1 tablespoon of aioli on the top bun and cap it off. Repeat with your other burgers. Eat immediately.

BAR TARTINE BURGER

Starting in 2009, I was the chef at Bar Tartine, a San Francisco bistro owned by Chad Robertson and Liz Prueitt. The burger at Bar Tartine was the beginning of a burger mantra: *thoughtful, reductive simplicity*. Here's what I mean by that phrase. There are a finite number of components in a burger. Meat, bread, vegetables, condiments, maybe cheese. Pursuing a better burger requires considering each individual component and making it the best possible version of itself. It was at Bar Tartine that I started honing in on each of the individual components. I became an agent in the creation of the ingredients: making the precise pickles I wanted, using aged beef, experimenting with a cheddar-mayo, and using buns baked daily from Tartine Bakery.

1½ pounds freshly ground grass-fed beef

½ onion, cut into ¼-inch rings

1 teaspoon sherry vinegar

Kosher salt

4 Brioche Buns (page 226 or store-bought)

2 tablespoons unsalted butter, at room temperature, plus another 2 teaspoons if using a stove top to cook the burgers

2 heads Little Gem lettuce

½ cup sliced dill pickles (page 64 or store-bought)

¼ cup mayonnaise (page 216 or store-bought)

SERVES 4

Divide the beef into four 6-ounce balls, handling minimally. Put a sheet of plastic wrap over a 4-inch ring mold on a cutting board or other hard surface. Put a ball in the middle of the mold and gently press down with the palm of your hand, forming a patty that is 4 inches wide. Pop it out with the plastic wrap. Put the patties on a large dish or small baking sheet and refrigerate until ready to cook.

In a cast-iron pan or on a grill over high heat, cook the onion slices until charred on both sides, 2 to 3 minutes. Remove from the heat, transfer to a small bowl, and toss with the sherry vinegar. Set aside.

Salt both sides of each patty.

Before you begin cooking the burgers, get the buns toasting. Heat a cast-iron skillet or similar surface over medium-low heat. Slice the buns in half horizontally. Smear the 2 tablespoons of butter on the buns and place, butter side down, on the hot surface, working in batches if necessary. Toast until golden brown, 6 to 8 minutes, adjusting the heat if necessary. You want to do your best to time their completion to the burger cooking.

While the buns toast, cook the patties.

To cook on a grill: Cook the patties over high heat for 2 minutes, then flip and cook for another 2 minutes, until medium-rare.

To cook on a stove top: Heat a large cast-iron pan over high heat. Spread ½ teaspoon of butter on the bottom of each patty. Add the patties and cook for 2 minutes, then flip and cook for another 2 minutes, until medium-rare.

Place a heaping forkful of onions and pickles on a bottom bun and top with a patty and several big leaves of lettuce. Spread 1 tablespoon of mayonnaise on the top bun and cap it off. Repeat with your other burgers. Eat immediately.

PICKLE-BRINED FRIED CHICKEN

Because everyone wants to spend two days making a fried chicken sandwich.

Okay, so this burger may require a bit of planning, but the ends justify the means. You've likely heard of fried chicken that has been soaked in buttermilk. This rendition takes that a little further: before it gets that buttermilk soak, the chicken spends several hours in a pickle juice, such as one leftover from a jar or two of dill pickles. (Pro Tip: Don't ever throw away pickle juice.)

The peppery coleslaw adds an acidic crunch. Another route is to serve the sandwiches with a ranch dressing (page 219) and bread and butter pickles (page 223), especially if made with green tomatoes. For a simpler alternative, go with your favorite hot sauce (Tabasco, Crystal, Texas Pete) and the best honey you can get your hands on. Try it with biscuits (page 230).

4 boneless chicken thighs (I like skin-on, but the more common skinless works fine)

3 cups dill pickle juice (page 64 or store-bought; enough to submerge the chicken thighs)

3 cups buttermilk (enough to submerge the chicken thighs)

BLACK PEPPER SLAW

½ head green cabbage, cored and sliced

1 tablespoon sherry vinegar

1 teaspoon honey

1 teaspoon kosher salt

1 teaspoon Urfa, Marash, or Aleppo chile flakes

½ teaspoon freshly ground black pepper

2 cups all-purpose flour

2 tablespoons cornstarch

1 tablespoon freshly ground black pepper

Kosher salt

8 cups rice bran oil, for frying

4 Pain de Mie Buns (page 62 or store-bought)

2 tablespoons unsalted butter, at room temperature

SERVES 4

In a large bowl or jar, fully submerge the chicken thighs in dill pickle juice. Cover and refrigerate for at least 6 hours, or up to 24 hours.

Remove the chicken thighs from the pickle juice, and then fully submerge them in the buttermilk in a second large bowl or jar. Cover and refrigerate. Let the chicken soak for at least 1 hour, or up to 12 hours.

To make the slaw: On the day you fry the chicken, put the cabbage in a large bowl. Add the vinegar, honey, salt, chile flakes, and pepper and toss until combined. Let sit while you fry the chicken.

When ready to fry the chicken, stir together the flour, cornstarch, pepper, and 1 teaspoon salt in a large bowl. Remove the chicken from the buttermilk, then dredge the chicken in the flour mixture, turning it to completely coat.

In a Dutch oven or heavy pot, heat the oil to 345°F over high heat. (If you're a beginning fryer, it's probably best to fry one thigh at a time; once you get the hang of it, you can try doing more at once.) Fry the chicken until it's golden brown or it reaches an internal temperature of 165°F, about 6 to 8 minutes. Adjust the heat as needed to maintain the temperature at 325°F. Using a spider skimmer or other small strainer, remove the chicken from the oil and drain on paper towels. Sprinkle with salt as desired.

While the chicken rests, toast the buns. Heat a cast-iron skillet or similar surface over high heat. Slice the buns in half horizontally. Smear the butter on the buns and place, butter side down, on the hot surface, working in batches if necessary. Toast until golden brown, 2 to 3 minutes.

Place a large handful of the coleslaw on a bottom bun and top with a chicken thigh. Be sure not to put a mountain of slaw on the sandwich; you want just enough to add some crunch and acid to the fried chicken. Cap it off. Repeat with your other sandwiches. Eat immediately.

Other Burgers

PORK BURGER

This is exactly like a hamburger except it's made with pork instead of beef. And instead of mayo, it's pork. And instead of pickles and onions, it's pickled pork and crunchy pork.

Grinding pork shoulder is the best way to go here, but if you buy ground pork, opt for the freshly ground version (ask your friendly neighborhood butcher). Avoid frozen prepackaged pork if possible. Pork skin is available in most of those aforementioned friendly neighborhood butcher shops. In the spring, fava leaves or pea greens can be used in place of red-leaf lettuce. A few greens cut through the pork—and just might make you feel like this burger is vaguely healthful and seasonal.

1½ pounds boneless pork shoulder

4 Pain de Mie Buns (page 62 or store-bought)

2 tablespoons unsalted butter, at room temperature

Salt

8 strips bacon, cooked

1 cup Pickled Pork Skin (recipe follows), thinly sliced

4 red-leaf lettuce leaves

4 tablespoons Pork Mayo (recipe follows) or store-bought mayo

SERVES 4

Cut the pork shoulder into 1-inch cubes; do not trim the fat. Chill the pork cubes and all detachable grinder parts in the freezer until the pork is firm to the touch, 15 to 20 minutes. When the pork is firm, pass it through the grinder—preferably the same grind coarseness as the Kronnerburger (page 47): ³⁄₁₆ inch.

Divide the pork into four equal balls. Put a sheet of plastic wrap over a 4-inch ring mold on a cutting board or other hard surface. Put a ball in the middle of the mold and gently press down with the palm of your hand, forming a patty that is 4 inches wide.

Pop it out with the plastic wrap. Put the patties on a large dish or small baking sheet and refrigerate until ready to cook.

Before you begin cooking the burgers, get the buns toasting. Heat a cast-iron skillet or similar surface over medium-low heat. Slice the buns horizontally. Smear the butter on the buns and place, butter side down, on the hot surface, working in batches if necessary. Toast until golden brown, 6 to 8 minutes, adjusting the heat if necessary. You want to do your best to time their completion to the burger cooking.

While the buns toast, cook the patties. Heat a skillet over high heat. Salt both sides of each patty and put them on the hot skillet. Cook until caramelized on one side, about 2 minutes, then flip the patties and cook until medium, 2 to 3 minutes.

Stack two strips of bacon, broken into segments, and ¼ cup pickled pork skin on a bottom bun and top with a patty and a lettuce leaf. Spread 1 tablespoon pork mayo on the top bun and cap it off. Repeat with your other burgers. Eat immediately.

PICKLED PORK SKIN

1 (4-ounce) strip raw pork skin (aka pork rind), about 6 by 6 inches

2 cups cider vinegar

2 teaspoons sugar

2 teaspoons kosher salt

1 teaspoon freshly ground black pepper

8 black peppercorns

4 whole cloves

1 white onion, thinly sliced

MAKES ABOUT 1 CUP

Bring a pot of water to a rolling boil over high heat. Add the pork skin and cook until soft, about 1 hour. When tender, like a soggy slice of bacon, drain the pork skin and cut it into thin strips, about ½ inch wide. The texture will be similar to al dente pasta. Return to the empty pot.

Add the vinegar, fully submerging the pork skin. Add the sugar, salt, ground pepper, peppercorns, and cloves. Stir to combine and bring to a simmer over medium-high heat.

Meanwhile, put the onion in a sealable container, preferably a jar or plastic quart container.

Once the vinegar mixture reaches a simmer, pour the entire mixture over the onion. If using immediately, let cool until the liquid is at room temperature. Otherwise, cover and store in the refrigerator for up to 1 month.

PORK MAYO

8 strips bacon, or ¼ cup lard

4 egg yolks

¼ cup cider vinegar

2 teaspoons mustard powder

2 cloves garlic, chopped

1 tablespoon honey

1 teaspoon kosher salt

1 teaspoon freshly ground black pepper

1 cup neutral oil (such as safflower oil)

MAKES 1½ CUPS

First, cook the bacon to get the bacon fat. (If using store-bought lard, skip this step.) Cook the bacon in a skillet over medium heat to your preferred level; I prefer crispy on one side. When done, let the bacon drain on paper towels and reserve for a burger topping; reserve the rendered bacon fat.

Combine the egg yolks, vinegar, mustard powder, garlic, honey, salt, and pepper in a food processor and process until combined. With the processor running, slowly add the oil, followed by the bacon fat (or lard) and process until emulsified, about 30 seconds. Store in an airtight container in the refrigerator for 1 to 2 weeks.

Other Burgers

LAMB BURGER

I cooked in Uruguay for a short stint in a small beachside town with spotty refrigeration and sheep grazing on grasslands that overlooked the ocean. We regularly killed lambs in the morning and served them later the same day. In Uruguay, most meat is cooked slowly over the coals of a wood fire. The meat is smoky from the fire with a slight salinity due to the animals' proximity to the ocean.

Like those Uruguayan lamb dishes, this burger is smoky and salty and acidic. It is simple and straightforward—ground meat topped with a simple herb salad and a charred pepper—but thanks to the addition of grape leaves, it's a little bit unique, too. For a quick weeknight meal, ground lamb is readily available in butcher shops and specialty markets. Opt for freshly ground lamb if possible and avoid frozen prepackaged versions. This burger is especially good cooked over a wood fire.

HERB SALAD

2 shallots, thinly sliced

Juice of 1 lime

Kosher salt

½ cup rinsed and chopped salt-packed or brined grape leaves

½ cup fresh cilantro leaves and thin stems

¼ cup fresh mint leaves

¼ cup fresh tarragon leaves

½ cup chopped pistachios

1 teaspoon fish sauce

BURGER

1½ pounds boneless lamb shoulder

4 small gypsy peppers, or 1 large yellow bell pepper

2 tablespoons extra-virgin olive oil, or as needed

4 Pain de Mie Buns (page 62 or store-bought)

2 tablespoons unsalted butter, at room temperature

Kosher salt

¼ cup Calabrian Chile Mayonnaise (page 216)

SERVES 4

To make the herb salad: Combine the shallots, lime juice, and a pinch of salt in a small bowl. Let sit to macerate for 15 minutes.

Meanwhile, combine the grape leaves, cilantro, mint, tarragon, pistachios, and fish sauce in a second bowl. Just before serving, add the shallot mixture and toss to combine.

To make the burger: Cut the lamb shoulder into 1-inch cubes; do not trim the fat. Chill the lamb cubes and all detachable grinder parts in the freezer until the pork is firm to the touch, 15 to 20 minutes. When the lamb is firm, pass it through the grinder with a ³⁄₁₆-inch grinder plate.

Divide the lamb into four equal balls. Put a sheet of plastic wrap over a 4-inch ring mold on a cutting board or other hard surface. Put a ball in the middle of the mold and gently press down with the palm of your hand, forming a patty that is 4 inches wide. Pop it out with the plastic wrap. Put the patties on a large dish or small baking sheet and refrigerate until ready to cook.

In a bowl, toss the peppers in the olive oil. Place the gypsy peppers over a grill or stove-top burner and cook, rotating occasionally with tongs, until roasted and blistered but not burned, 3 to 5 minutes. Set aside. When cool enough to handle, remove the tops. Cut a slit in each pepper, open it up, and remove the seeds. Set the peppers aside. (If using a bell pepper, cut into quarters vertically and remove the ribs and seeds.)

Before you begin cooking the burgers, get the buns toasting. Heat a cast-iron skillet or similar surface over medium-low heat. Slice the buns in half horizontally. Smear the butter on the buns and place, butter side down, on the hot surface, working in batches if necessary. Toast until golden brown, 6 to 8 minutes, adjusting the heat if necessary. You want to do your best to time their completion to the burger cooking.

While the buns toast, cook the patties. Heat a cast-iron skillet over high heat. Salt both sides of each patty and put them on the hot skillet. Cook on one side, about 2 minutes, then flip the patties and cook until medium-rare, 2 to 3 minutes, or longer if desired.

Place a pepper on a bottom bun and top with a patty and some herb salad. Spread 1 tablespoon chile mayonnaise on the top bun and cap it off. Repeat with your other burgers. Eat immediately.

SHRIMP BURGER

A burger, at its best, is a beautifully simple composition of sensations: crunch, creaminess, acidity, richness, hot, cold. Once you understand the basic elements—or find an equation that you prefer—tasty variations abound.

To wit, the standard Kronnerburger is anchored by a beef patty that is accentuated by crunch (iceberg lettuce, onion), creaminess (cheddar mayo), acidity (pickles), and a touch of sweetness (a pain de mie bun, and, when in season, a slice of fresh tomato). The Kronnerburger has many spin-offs, all of which follow a similar formula. You'll see it everywhere, whether it's the Earth Burger (yuba bacon for crunch, tofu mayo for creaminess) or the Lamb Burger (herb salad for acid, gypsy peppers for sweetness) or this one, the Shrimp Burger, with its sweet-acidic barbecue sauce and crunchy pickles. Once you know what to look for, you can't un-see it. And hopefully when you're building your own burgers, you'll remember to check off the very same boxes.

1 large (about 1 pound) sweet potato

2 tablespoons plus 1 teaspoon neutral oil (such as safflower oil)

1 pound (about 40 medium) shrimp, peeled and deveined

Kosher salt

1 bunch chives, chopped

4 Pain de Mie Buns (page 62 or store-bought)

2 tablespoons unsalted butter, at room temperature

¼ cup potato starch

12 to 16 bread and butter pickle slices (page 223 or store-bought)

4 to 6 iceberg lettuce leaves

¼ cup Jalapeño Barbecue Sauce (recipe follows)

SERVES 4

Preheat the oven to 425°F.

Wrap the sweet potato in aluminum foil and roast until soft but not mushy, 50 to 60 minutes. A fork should be able to easily penetrate it. Let cool. When cool enough to handle, chop the sweet potato into large chunks, peeling off (but reserving) the skins. Set aside.

Heat 1 teaspoon of the oil in a sauté pan over high heat. Add the shrimp and a large pinch of salt, stir, and cook until pink, about 1 minute. Transfer to a food processor, add the sweet potato skins, and process until the shrimp mixture is a coarse texture, about 10 seconds. (The skins add a nice textural component to the final product.)

Transfer the shrimp mixture to a large bowl. Add the flesh of the sweet potato, crumbling it with your fingers as it falls into the bowl. Add the chives and, using your hands, mix until fully incorporated.

Divide the shrimp mixture into four equal portions and form into tightly packed balls. Put a sheet of plastic wrap over a 4-inch ring mold on a cutting board or other hard surface. Put a ball in the middle of the mold and gently press down with the palm of your hand, forming a patty that is 4 inches wide. Pop it out with the plastic wrap. Put the patties on a large dish or small baking sheet, cover with plastic wrap, and put in the freezer until firm but not frozen, 15 to 20 minutes.

Before you begin cooking the burgers, get the buns toasting. Heat a cast-iron skillet or similar surface over medium-low heat. Slice the buns in half horizontally. Smear the butter on the buns and place, butter side down, on the hot surface, working in batches if necessary. Toast until golden brown, 6 to 8 minutes, adjusting the heat if necessary. You want to do your best to time their completion to the burger cooking.

While the buns toast, cook the patties. Stir together the potato starch with 2 teaspoons salt in a bowl. One at a time, dredge the patties in the mixture, turning to evenly coat. (This will help maintain integrity during cooking.) In a skillet, heat the remaining 2 tablespoons oil over medium-high heat, making sure you have about ⅛ inch of oil. Add the patties to the skillet and cook until golden brown, about 5 minutes on each side.

Place a patty on a bottom bun and top with the pickles and lettuce. Spread 1 tablespoon barbecue sauce on the top bun and cap it off. Repeat with your other burgers. Eat immediately.

JALAPEÑO BARBECUE SAUCE

1 teaspoon neutral oil (such as safflower oil)
1 white onion, sliced
1 cup sliced pickled jalapeños or Quick Pickled Chiles (page 223)
¼ cup honey

MAKES ¾ CUP

Heat the oil in a skillet or sauté pan over medium-high heat. Add the onion and sauté until soft and slightly brown, 5 to 6 minutes. Add the jalapeños and stir to combine; cook another 1 to 2 minutes, until the jalapeños are warmed through. Transfer to a food processor or blender and process until smooth. Add the honey and pulse, just to combine. Set aside and refrigerate until ready to use. Keeps for 1 week, refrigerated.

HAND-CUT BURGER

No grinder? No problem. My friend Michael Black, a San Francisco sushi chef, once told me that the only burger worth eating is the one you cut by hand. A hand-cut burger is a nice option for a smaller group, or a sophisticated dinner party where you can sing the praises of beef tallow. This recipe magically turns a single steak into dinner for four.

1 (1½-pound) boneless rib-eye steak (preferably dry-aged)

2 cups unsalted butter or rendered beef tallow, plus 2 tablespoons unsalted butter, at room temperature

1 white onion, cut crosswise into ½-inch rings

1 (5-ounce) piece horseradish (2 to 3 inches), finely grated

2 tablespoons buttermilk

Kosher salt

4 Pain de Mie Buns (page 62) or 8 slices soft slab bread

16 to 24 dill pickle slices (page 64 or store-bought)

SERVES 4

Chill the steak in the freezer until firm to the touch but not frozen, 15 to 20 minutes. Cut the steak into ¼-inch-thick slices, then slice into ¼-inch-thick strips, and then into ¼-inch cubes. Remove the sinew and connective tissue but keep the fat.

Divide the beef into four equal balls. Put a sheet of plastic wrap over a 4-inch ring mold on a cutting board or other hard surface. Put a ball in the middle of the mold and gently press down with the palm of your hand, forming a patty that is 4 inches wide. Pop it out with the plastic wrap. Put the patties on a large dish or small baking sheet and refrigerate until ready to cook.

Melt 2 cups of the butter in a pot over medium heat. (Why yes, that is a lot of butter, but it's used to fully submerge the onion while it cooks; you will not eat

2 cups of butter in this burger.) Add the onion, turn the heat to low, and gently cook at a bare simmer until the onion is tender, about 20 minutes. The onion should be cooked but still al dente, so there's some texture and a slight hit of sharpness yet not enough that you'll taste onion the rest of the day. Remove the onion from the butter and drain on a paper towel.

While the onion cooks, make a horseradish sauce. In a bowl, mix the grated horseradish with the buttermilk and a pinch of salt. Stir to combine and refrigerate until ready to use.

Before you begin cooking the burgers, get the buns toasting. Heat a cast-iron skillet or similar surface over medium-low heat. Slice the buns in half horizontally. Smear the remaining 2 tablespoons of butter on the buns and place, butter side down, on the hot surface, working in batches if necessary. Toast until golden brown, 6 to 8 minutes, adjusting the heat if necessary. You want to do your best to time their completion to the burger cooking.

While the buns toast, cook the patties. Heat a cast-iron skillet or grill over high heat. Use a spatula to handle the patty—it will be loose, so be careful. Salt both sides of each patty and put them on the hot skillet. Cook on one side, about 1 minute, then flip the patties and cook until rare, another minute.

Place a patty on a bottom bun and top with some pickles and onions. Slather 1½ teaspoons horseradish sauce on the top bun and cap it off. Repeat.

RAWBURGER
(SERVED RAW)

The Rawburger was born of necessity. Once upon a time, I needed to serve burgers—in some form—for a party in a house where I couldn't cook anything. The result? The tartare burger, using the remixed ingredients from the Kronnerburger. Turns out it's pretty damn delicious. The building blocks of France's traditional beef tartare are all there—maybe not in actual ingredients but in the roles they play. Swap in a dollop of aged cheddar mayo for the typical egg yolk and sub pickles and their juice for the acidic kick of Worcestershire. And the crostini? Those are just toasted slices of burger buns.

It should be obvious but you definitely don't want to use crappy supermarket ground beef for any raw meat dish. Splurge for the good stuff, from a good cow, ideally dry-aged. If you can, grind it yourself, or at the very least, use freshly ground beef.

2 to 3 buns or 3 to 4 slices of similar bread

1 tablespoon unsalted butter

8 ounces freshly ground, dry-aged beef (preferably ³⁄₁₆-inch grind)

¼ cup diced Charred Onion, cold (page 65)

¼ cup diced dill pickle (page 64 or store-bought), plus sliced dill pickles for serving

2 teaspoons dill pickle juice

½ teaspoon Chinese hot mustard, plus more for serving

½ teaspoon kosher salt

1 tablespoon Cheddar Mayonnaise (page 65) or store-bought mayonnaise

SERVES 2 AS A STARTER

Cut the bun vertically into thin slices. Melt the butter in a sauté pan over medium-high heat. Add the bun slices and toast until nice and crispy on both sides, about 5 minutes. Let cool. Voilà, now you have crostini.

Combine the ground beef, onion, diced pickle, pickle juice, mustard, and salt in a large bowl and, using a spoon, gently mix until fully incorporated. Add the cheddar mayonnaise and mix again.

Place the mixture on a nice serving platter or large plate. Serve as a shared appetizer with the toasted pain de mie, with sliced pickles and additional mustard on the side. Encourage eaters to add the pickles and mustards to the toasts as desired.

Other Burgers

CHAPTER 4 BURGER SIDES

ONION RINGS

I have sworn to never make another goddamned onion ring again for as long as I live literally hundreds of times. I have heard similar pronouncements uttered by quite a few fellow cooks working beside me over the years. I have seen cooks go down in flames trying to keep up with a seemingly insurmountable number of onion ring orders. I have tried to devise ways to stop serving onion rings to prevent kitchen swearing. I have even tried to pre-batter onion rings to simplify their cooking process. It has all been in vain.

We still serve lots of onion rings, they are still battered to order, and, fortunately, everyone is still alive. At their worst, onion rings are a messy, temperamental mess. At their best, onion rings are a lighter-than-air meditation on the nuances of fried food.

Originally, I made onion rings with beer and a bit of wheat flour, but after a dear friend and mentor expressed her dismay at not being able to enjoy them because of the wheat, I made the recipe gluten-free by using sparkling water and rice flour. The result is so far superior to the original version I haven't looked back since. It is light and glassy in all the right ways. This batter works very well for basically any veggie you see fit to fry, so venture beyond onions. The possibilities are endless.

There are several important elements to consider to achieve the best possible results with this recipe. The first is that the rings receive a very light and even coating of starch prior to being battered. Make sure there are not any clumps attached to the rings as these will create uncooked pockets of batter that will be unpleasant to eat. The second is that the batter must be the right consistency; it should be the thickness of pancake batter and should coat the onions as thinly and evenly as possible. You want each ring completely covered, without any excess batter.

Use a small pair of tongs to work with one ring at a time, especially if you're an onion ring beginner, going from the dredge to the batter to the oil. It is very important to use fresh oil and not to crowd the frying vessel in order to prevent the rings from sticking together or steaming instead of frying.

CONTINUED

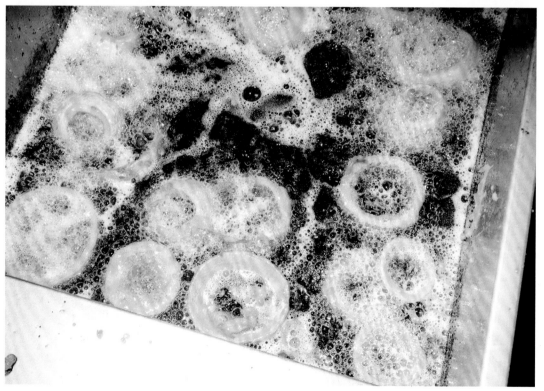

2 cups rice flour

2 tablespoons potato starch

2 tablespoons cornstarch

1 teaspoon paprika

Kosher salt

1¾ cups sparkling water

2 white onions

4 to 8 cups rice bran oil or other neutral oil, for frying

Calabrian Chile Mayonnaise (page 216), for serving

SERVES 3 OR 4

In a large bowl, stir together the rice flour, potato starch, cornstarch, paprika, and a pinch of salt. Transfer ½ cup of the rice flour mixture to a second bowl. This second bowl is your dry dredge. Add the sparkling water to the large bowl, whisking until smooth; it should be saucy enough to coat the back of a spoon. This is your wet dredge.

Peel and cut the onions into ½-inch rings. Discard the three innermost rings. (Those are not rings; those are nubs. We save them for the caramelized onions used in the Patty Melt, page 74). Carefully separate each ring. Gently put the rings in the dry dredge, evenly coating them.

In a Dutch oven or heavy pot, heat the oil over high heat to 375°F, making sure you have 2 inches of oil. Working with one ring at a time, dip the dredged onion rings into the wet dredge. The batter should coat the onion ring, but not be heavy or gloppy. When the oil hits 375°F, fry the onions until golden brown, about 90 seconds, working in batches if needed to make sure the onion rings don't touch each other. Adjust the heat as needed to maintain the oil temperature at 355°F. Using a spider skimmer or other small strainer, remove the onions rings from the oil and let drain on paper towels. Sprinkle with salt as desired. Serve with Calabrian Chile Mayonnaise. Eat immediately.

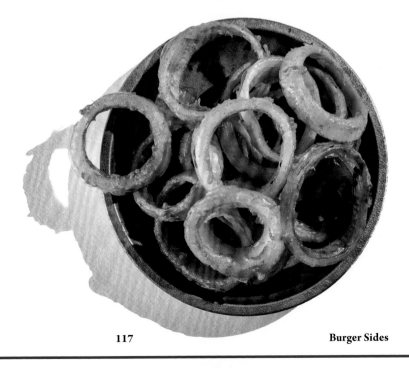

FRENCH FRIES

French fries are sort of like burgers, in that everyone has his or her own favorite style. Shoestring, curly, waffle-cut, and so on. There are plenty of recipes out there, each with tiny tweaks that can make a big difference in the final product. Yet all fries consist simply of potatoes and seasoning (usually just salt). Potatoes and salt—that's it. The cooking methodology, however, is the thing of note.

Whereas burger preferences can run the gamut from crusty thin patties to beefy steak-house numbers, most people can agree on the basic components that make fries stand out: flavor and, above all, texture. Unless you're a monster who enjoys the mushy species that is waffle fries, just about everyone can agree that the best fries—be it steak fries or McDonald's fries—all have hot, crackling shells with soft, custardy interiors.

There are several ways to achieve fry nirvana. The best way, as you'll see in the coming pages, involves Kennebec potatoes that are fried, frozen, and then fried a second time. Though it's a straightforward process, it does take a little more time than preparing your average bag of frozen fries.

So you can't find Kennebec potatoes in your local grocery store? First of all, that sucks, because Kennebecs are, by far, the best potato for fries. However, though Kennebecs are a common sight in restaurants, they remain curiously rare in grocery stores. Assuming you don't want to go to another store or scour the Internet for further potato options, as one does, you've still got a few paths.

The more ubiquitous russet potatoes also retain their crispiness when fried and are the best substitute, especially for Easy Way Fries (page 120). Red potatoes also fry nicely but the final texture is a bit off, with the interior tending less toward creamy and more toward mealy. Yukon gold potatoes are my pick for the best flavor—a vibrant potato essence, if you will—but they tend to be a little chewier so you won't get that glasslike exterior snap. And if all else fails, you've got onion rings.

CONTINUED

LAZY WAY FRIES

Go to the supermarket. Wander the frozen food aisle, taking care not to make eye contact with any of the cows on the Ben and Jerry's ice cream cartons. Resist the temptation of the taquitos and the siren song of the stromboli. Keep moving toward your destination: that crinkly bag of frozen fries. Choose one made with Kennebec potatoes, if possible, and certainly one with minimal additives. The only ingredient you need is potato. Exit the frozen section. Perhaps pick up some ketchup on the way to the register. Pay for your goods. Once home, follow the instructions on the bag. Relish the flashback to your childhood, when your favorite aunt would heat up these fries in the oven. Now you're really home.

EASY WAY FRIES

Boiling potatoes before frying them is a shortcut to making decent fries at home. Compared with Best Way Fries (page 121), this version takes a fraction of the time—about 30 minutes—and is the best way to fry russets. Pro-Tip: If you're not eating them right away, hold the completed fries in a 275°F oven.

Kosher salt

1 pound russet potatoes

4 cups rice bran oil or other neutral oil, for frying

SERVES 3 OR 4

Bring a large pot of salted water to a boil over high heat.

Cut the potatoes, with the skin on, into flat ½-inch slices. Then take the slabs and cut them into ½-inch spears. (The exact thickness is entirely up to you and your fry preferences, but take care to cut them evenly.)

Gently add the potatoes to the boiling water, lower the heat to medium, and gently simmer until soft, about 20 minutes, or slightly longer depending on the thickness of your spears. You want them to be soggy and almost falling apart.

Using a spider skimmer or other small strainer, remove the potatoes from the water. Handle gently because they will be fragile. Drain in a colander and pat dry.

In a Dutch oven or heavy pot, heat the oil to 365°F over high heat. Working in two batches if necessary, fry the potatoes until golden brown, about 2 minutes. Adjust the heat as needed to maintain the oil temperature at 345°F. Using a spider skimmer or other small strainer, remove the fries from the oil and drain on paper towels. Sprinkle with salt as desired. Eat immediately.

BEST WAY FRIES

It is known: the best fries are made with Kennebec potatoes that are fried at a low temperature, frozen, and then fried at a high temperature. Don't dispute facts.

1 pound potatoes (preferably Kennebec)
4 cups rice bran oil or other neutral oil, for frying
Kosher salt

SERVES 3 OR 4

Cut the potatoes, with the skin on, into flat ½-inch slices. Then take the slabs and cut them into ½-inch spears. (The exact thickness is entirely up to you and your fry preferences, but take care to cut them evenly.) Once cut, put the potatoes in a bowl and rinse under cold running water until the water is clear. Drain in a colander and pat dry.

In a Dutch oven or heavy pot, heat the oil to 345°F over medium-high heat. Working in two batches if necessary, fry the potatoes until fully cooked through, about 3½ minutes. Adjust the heat as needed to maintain the oil temperature at 325°F. This first fry is more of an oil blanching, so the fries shouldn't take on much color; they will be blond. Using a spider skimmer or other small strainer, remove the fries from the oil and drain on paper towels. Transfer to a rimmed baking sheet that will fit in your freezer.

Put the potatoes in the freezer and keep them there until frozen solid, about 6 hours. (Covered, they can stay in the freezer indefinitely.)

When ready to finish the fries, reheat the oil to 395°F over high heat. Working in two batches if necessary, fry the frozen fries until deep golden brown, about 7 minutes. Adjust the heat as needed to maintain the oil temperature at 375°F. Using a spider skimmer or other small strainer, remove the fries from the oil and drain on paper towels. Sprinkle with salt as desired. Eat immediately.

HOW TO (SAFELY AND EASILY) DEEP-FRY THINGS

Frying at home can be exhilarating but also dangerous, so becoming comfortable with hot oil is a crucial step to creating fries and onion rings. Fortunately, some basic tips can ensure that there are no disasters.

1. Use a frying thermometer. It's extremely helpful, if not crucial, to know how hot your oil is. This will make everything easier, especially for the recipes in this book, which refer to specific temperatures during the frying process. Other recommended equipment: a metal spider skimmer, slotted spoon, or other small strainer to remove the fried food from the hot oil.

2. Use a heavy pot, like a Dutch oven—the heavier, the better—as it will help the oil to maintain a consistent temperature.

3. Size matters! The diameter of your pot determines how much oil you will need for proper frying. Different pots require different amounts of oil. A good rule of thumb: You want enough oil to fully submerge the food, which means you want the oil to be at least 3 inches deep. Never fill a pot more than halfway. In a standard Dutch oven, this usually amounts to 4 cups or so.

4. Use the right type of oil. I prefer rice bran oil because it is good for high-heat frying and it comes from relatively sustainable sources. Peanut oil is the best alternative, and second (and third) best are non-GMO, expeller-pressed safflower and canola oils.

5. Don't be afraid to get the oil hotter than your desired frying temperature. When you add the food to the hot oil, the temperature will likely drop about 20°F, so you actually want the temperature to be a bit hotter before frying. In other words, if you want to cook your potatoes at 375°F, you'll want to heat the oil to 395°F.

6. Carefully lower the foods into the hot oil—don't toss them in. Speaking of which . . .

7. Unless you are immune to the splatter of hot oil, one of those splatter-screen frying-pan covers is rather helpful, just in case.

8. Don't crowd the pot. The fried foods should be bubbling quickly and actively. If you put too many foods in at once, the oil temperature will plummet, which means that the food won't fry immediately and will ultimately get soggy.

9. Drain freshly fried foods on paper towels or on a rack set inside a pan.

10. Do not reuse oil that has a bunch of detritus floating around or has been used repeatedly. For the recipes in this book, one batch of oil should be able to withstand two full recipes.

11. Pay attention! Frying successfully at home means monitoring the temperature of the oil and adjusting it up or down moment by moment.

STEAK FRIES

Steak fries are a polarizing genre of fries, perhaps even more polarizing than their crinkle-cut brethren. At their best, they can be an exemplar of potato-ness, simultaneously giving you the best of a both french fries and baked potatoes: a crusty, addictive structure around a soft and meaty interior. At their worst, they are mealy and bland and textureless potato shapes. Fortunately, *these* steak fries are the good version. Even more convenient for those of you who may be averse to bubbling oil, these fries are baked.

Kosher salt
3 russet potatoes
1 tablespoon neutral oil (such as safflower oil)
Freshly ground black pepper

SERVES 3 OR 4

Bring a large pot of salted water to a boil over high heat.

Meanwhile, quarter the potatoes lengthwise and then cut each quarter into two or three wedges.

Carefully add the potato wedges to the boiling water, lower the heat to medium, and gently simmer until soft and a fork can easily go through them, 10 to 15 minutes. Using a spider skimmer

or other small strainer, remove the fries from the water. Pat dry and let cool.

Preheat the oven to 400°F.

Combine the potato wedges and the oil on a large rimmed baking sheet, toss until evenly coated, and then spread out in a single layer. Bake until golden brown, about 15 minutes. Sprinkle with salt and pepper as desired. Eat immediately.

POTATO CHIPS

There's something psychologically rewarding about eating your own potato chips in your own house. In addition to snacking, these chips are also good with dips (see pages 133 to 136), and even in place of the fries in poutine (page 128).

2 russet potatoes
2 cups rice bran oil or other neutral oil, for frying
Kosher salt

SERVES 2 TO 4

Using a mandoline, thinly slice the potatoes; the thickness is entirely up to you. If you're going to eat the chips on their own, thinner is good; if you're eating them with a sturdy dip, go a little thicker. Once cut, put the potatoes in a bowl and rinse under cold running water until the water is clear.

In a Dutch oven or heavy pot, heat the oil to 300°F over high heat. Working in batches, fry the potatoes, gently stirring and agitating them in the oil so they fry evenly and don't stick to each other, until golden brown, 2 to 3 minutes. Adjust the heat as needed to maintain the oil temperature at 280°F. Using a spider skimmer or other small strainer, remove the chips from the oil and drain on paper towels. Let cool.

Season with salt as desired. Store in an airtight container. They will stay fresh for a few days.

VARIATION: BARBECUE CHIPS

The secret to adding smoky flavor to potato chips is—drum roll, please—smoke. And, yes, you can skip the smoking step and just toss the chips with the seasoning mix and it'll still taste good.

1 teaspoon salt
½ teaspoon freshly ground black pepper
½ teaspoon paprika
¼ teaspoon sugar

After you fry the chips, transfer them to a container with a lid and follow the instructions for easy stove-top smoking on page 161. If you have a dedicated stove-top smoker, smoke the chips over smoking oak wood for 2 to 3 minutes. Once completed, remove the chips from the smoking apparatus and put in a large bowl.

Stir together the salt, pepper, paprika, and sugar in a small bowl. Sprinkle over the chips and toss gently to combine.

VARIATION: COOL RANCH CHIPS

1 tablespoon kosher salt
1 teaspoon ground celery seeds
1 teaspoon ground bay leaves
1 teaspoon ground fennel seeds
1 teaspoon dill weed
1 teaspoon mushroom seasoning (such as Po Lo Ku brand)
½ teaspoon citric acid
½ teaspoon sugar
½ teaspoon black pepper

Stir together the salt, ground celery, ground bay leaves, ground fennel, ground dill, mushroom seasoning, citric acid, sugar, and black pepper in a small bowl. Sprinkle over the chips while they are still hot from cooking and toss gently to combine.

SWEET POTATO TOTS

The secret to these croquettelike tots is an equal distribution of cooked sweet potato and raw sweet potato. You owe it to your friends and family to make sweet potato tots. Come on, give them some of your tots.

2 medium (about 1 pound) sweet potatoes

2 teaspoons cornstarch

Kosher salt

3 to 4 cups rice bran oil or other neutral oil, for frying

SERVES 3 OR 4

Preheat the oven to 425°F.

Wrap one sweet potato in aluminum foil and roast until very soft, 30 to 45 minutes. Remove from the oven and let cool.

Meanwhile, shred the remaining sweet potato on the large holes of a box grater.

In a large bowl, combine the soft interior of the cooked sweet potato and the raw sweet potato. Add the cornstarch and ½ teaspoon salt and, using a wooden spoon or your hands, combine thoroughly to create a uniform mixture. Form individual tots with your hands, rolling them into rounds; I like mine the size of golf balls, but others may prefer a smaller, more traditional size, the width of postage stamps.

If you have time, freeze the tots for the best results. Transfer the tots to a rimmed baking sheet that will fit in your freezer. Freeze the tots until frozen solid, 20 to 30 minutes. (Covered, they will keep frozen indefinitely.)

When ready to finish the tots, heat the oil to 370°F over high heat. Working in batches, fry the tots until golden brown, 3 to 4 minutes for unfrozen tots and about 5 minutes for frozen tots. The exterior should be crispy, and the interior should be warmed through and creamy. Adjust the heat as needed to maintain the oil temperature at 350°F. Using a spider skimmer or other small strainer, remove the tots from the oil and drain on paper towels. Sprinkle with salt. Eat immediately.

FRENCH FRY PAVÉ

This is what happens if you turn scalloped potatoes into scalloped fries. Dishes like scalloped potatoes and potato gratin feature thinly sliced disks of potato layered atop one another to create a wonderfully textured casserole. But that same design—myriad layers of potatoes, sans gratin's usual creamy components—also yields a great fried version.

These fries—let's call them French fry pavé, a reference to a classic French technique—start the same way as scalloped potatoes: by assembling layers of potatoes and then baking them. But then, the potatoes get pressed and refrigerated, with the goal of creating a dense, layered terrine. The block is then sliced and fried. When choosing the vessel, opt for a small, deep, and rectangular baking dish that can easily fit a weight on top, such as a similar-size baking dish. The result is shatteringly crunchy and flaky.

2½ to 3 pounds russet potatoes
Kosher salt
4 cups rice bran oil or other neutral oil, for frying

SERVES 4

Preheat the oven to 300°F.

Line a rimmed baking sheet with parchment paper or coat an ovenproof baking dish with a vegetable oil spray.

Using a mandoline, thinly slice the potatoes. The disks should be thin enough that you can see light through them. Don't rinse them; unlike with potato chips, the starch is a valuable component here.

Place the potato slices in a small, rectangular, and high-walled baking dish, one at a time, slightly overlapping with its neighbor. Working quickly to avoid oxidation, layer the potatoes in an organized way, but don't be too obsessive about it. Fill the dish one layer at a time. Add a pinch of salt every third layer or so.

Cover very tightly with aluminum foil, making sure it's airtight to enable steaming. Bake until tender, about 1 hour.

Remove the foil and plastic and let cool. When cool, cover with parchment paper and use a similar-size pan or dish to weight it down. If possible, place something heavy in the second dish to increase the weight.

Refrigerate for at least 6 hours, or up to overnight.

When ready to fry, cut the pavé into shoestrings or spears. The thickness and shape is entirely up to you, but I like my pavé fries to be about ¼ by ¼ by 4 inches.

In a Dutch oven or heavy pot, heat the oil to 365°F over high heat. Working in batches, gently add several fries into the oil and fry until golden brown, about 2 minutes. Adjust the heat as needed to maintain the oil temperature at 345°F. Using a spider skimmer or other small strainer, remove the fries from the oil and drain on paper towels. Sprinkle with salt as desired. Eat immediately.

GLUTEN FREEDOM FRIES WITH FREEDOM GRAVY
(AKA POUTINE)

Are you tired of the world? Of your job? Of social media? This stew can't solve all your problems but the aroma of warm spices that will fill your kitchen will be a nice escape for a few hours.

In the restaurant, we pour this gravy over fries and cheese curds for our version of poutine, but it's also good over rice or even on its own. This recipe will work with nearly any combination of bone-in beef cuts, but the shank works particularly well.

2 pounds bone-in beef shank

1 pound boneless beef cheeks

Kosher salt

3 tablespoons unsalted butter or rendered beef tallow

2 carrots, peeled and diced

1 white onion, diced

1 celery rib, diced

½ fennel bulb, cored and diced

½ cup canned, peeled tomatoes in juice

4 cloves garlic, minced

¼ cup (about 2 ounces) salted anchovy fillets

1 cup dry red wine

2 star anise pods

1 teaspoon coriander seeds

½ teaspoon fennel seeds

½ teaspoon anise seeds

⅛ teaspoon celery seeds

⅛ teaspoon mustard seeds

10 whole cloves

2 allspice berries

2 bay leaves

1 arbol chile, or ⅛ teaspoon red pepper flakes

2 teaspoons mushroom seasoning (such as Po Lo Ku brand), or ⅛ teaspoon mushroom powder (optional, see page 82)

2 teaspoons freshly ground black pepper

10 cups beef stock or low-sodium beef broth, or as needed

¼ cup Worcestershire sauce

½ cup warm water

2 tablespoons cornstarch or potato starch

1 recipe hot french fries (page 118)

4 to 6 ounces cheese curds (optional; such as Spring Hill Jersey Cheese brand)

1 to 2 green onions, thinly cut on the bias

SERVES 4

Liberally season the beef shank and beef cheeks with salt, about 1 teaspoon for each side.

Melt the butter in a large stockpot over medium heat. Working in batches, add the meat and cook until well browned on all sides, flipping and rotating as necessary to get an even, thorough sear, about 10 minutes for each batch. You want the meat to get seriously caramelized; look for a crusty, bubbly exterior. Remove the meat from the pot and set aside.

Add the carrots, onion, celery, and fennel to the pot and cook, stirring occasionally, until the vegetables are browned, about 10 minutes. You want the onion, in particular, to be evenly caramelized. Add the tomatoes and their juice and cook, stirring occasionally, until slightly colored, about 2 minutes. Stir in the garlic and anchovies and cook for about 2 minutes. Pour in the wine and cook until reduced by a third, 5 to 7 minutes.

While the wine is reducing, prepare an herb sachet. Cut a small piece of a cheesecloth and fill it with

the star anise, coriander seeds, fennel seeds, anise seeds, celery seeds, mustard seeds, cloves, allspice berries, bay leaves, and chile. Tie it up with kitchen twine.

Once the wine has reduced, return the meat to the pot.

Preheat the oven to 200°F.

Add the herb sachet, mushroom seasoning, and pepper to the pot and then pour in the stock and Worcestershire. The meat should be fully submerged in the stock; if it isn't, add more beef stock (or water) as needed. Bring to a simmer,

then cover and transfer the pot to the oven. Cook until the meat is fall-apart tender, at least 4 hours.

Remove the pot from the oven and allow the stew to cool. Remove and shred the meat, discarding the bones and the herb sachet. In a small bowl, combine the ½ cup warm water and cornstarch and stir to create a slurry and then stir it into the pot. Heat the mixture and thicken the sauce. Return the meat to the pot and reheat. Pour over fries and cheese curds. Garnish with green onions and eat immediately.

Burger Sides

VEGAN CHILI–CHEESE FRIES

Do you want to enjoy the food that is normally reserved for monster truck rallies, darkened movie theaters, and carnivals within the confines of your own home? Are you sick of the government-subsidized beef industrial complex ruining all of your chili with feedlot castoffs? Make this party-size meat-free chili-cheese fries recipe and then go confront a lobbyist. Or don't. Who am I to tell you how to live?

VEGAN CHEESE

3 cups water

1½ cups cashews

1 russet potato, peeled and cut into chunks

¼ cup vegetable oil

3 tablespoons nutritional yeast

2 tablespoons cider vinegar

1½ teaspoons kosher salt

1 teaspoon paprika

1 teaspoon mustard powder

1 teaspoon onion powder

1 teaspoon garlic powder

½ teaspoon ground turmeric

CHILI

1 tablespoon smoked paprika

1 teaspoon ground cumin

1 to 2 teaspoons neutral oil (such as safflower oil)

8 ounces plant-based meat (such as a Beyond Burger), or 1⅓ cups cooked grains (such as quinoa, bulgur, farro)

Kosher salt

1 onion, diced

1 carrot, peeled and diced (about ½ cup)

4 dried mild chiles (such as guajillo or New Mexico; optional)

4 cloves garlic, sliced

2 cups fresh or canned diced tomatoes with their juices

1 jalapeño chile, chopped

3 cups vegetable stock or water

½ cup warm water

2 tablespoons cornstarch or potato starch

¼ cup cider vinegar

1 recipe french fries (page 118)

SERVES 6 TO 8

To make the vegan cheese: In a large pot, bring the water to a boil over high heat. When boiling, add the cashews and then turn off the heat. Let the cashews sit for 1 hour, then add the potato chunks and return to a boil over high heat. Lower to a simmer and cook until the potato is soft, about 15 minutes. Add the oil, nutritional yeast, vinegar, salt, paprika, mustard powder, onion powder, garlic powder, and turmeric. Stir and gently simmer until slightly thickened, another 5 minutes. Let cool slightly and then transfer to a blender and process until smooth. If not using immediately, store, covered, in the refrigerator. Will keep indefinitely.

To make the chili: Heat a small skillet over medium-high heat. Add the paprika and cumin and toast until fragrant, 1 to 2 minutes. Stir the spices often during toasting to be sure they don't burn. Set aside to cool.

If using plant-based meat, heat 1 teaspoon of the oil in a Dutch oven or stockpot over high heat. Add the plant-based meat and a pinch of salt and cook until browned, 3 to 4 minutes, breaking up the plant-based meat with a wooden spoon. Use the spoon to scrape up any browned bits from the bottom of a pan. Remove the meat from the pot and set aside.

Heat the pot over medium-high heat, and add the remaining 1 teaspoon oil if the pot is dry. Add the onion and carrot and cook until well browned, 5 to 7 minutes. Add the chiles, garlic, and toasted spices and sweat the garlic, 3 to 4 minutes. Add the tomatoes and their juices and the jalapeño and cook until slightly caramelized, 3 to 4 minutes. Add the stock, bring to a boil, and then turn the heat to low and simmer until thickened, about 30 minutes.

While the chili simmers, stir together the warm water and cornstarch in a small bowl to create a slurry. Add the slurry and plant-based meat or cooked grains and cook for an additional 15 minutes. Remove from the heat and stir in the vinegar. Cover to keep warm and then gently reheat the vegan cheese over low heat.

Spread the fries on a platter and ladle the chili and vegan cheese over the top. Eat immediately.

TARTARE

So you've got yourself a beautiful dry-aged grass-fed piece of beef, like a rib eye, a sirloin, a New York strip, or even a round. It is, paradoxically, at once firm and tender, chewy and smooth. It's everything that a dry-aged piece of meat can be.

When good beef is cut by hand like this, carefully into cubes, it's almost like the anti-tartare, the opposite of the mushy versions served at the saddest corner bistros. This rendition is clean and simple, a perfect pedestal for the beef itself, closer to sushi or poke than most ground beef tartare.

In this day and age, you probably won't find dry-aged chuck, let alone dry-aged ground beef, for burgers at your neighborhood market. However, dry-aged steaks are a different story. There's a much bigger demand for those sexy dry-aged cuts, like rib eyes and New Yorks, so it's more common to find them at decent butcher shops and good markets.

This straightforward tartare recipe gets an extra boost of beefiness from bone marrow, which is used to toast the bread crumbs. Ask your butcher to cut the raw bone in half to make it easier to extract the raw marrow.

6 ounces dry-aged beef steak (such as filet mignon, sirloin, or rib eye)

1 (2-inch) marrow bone, halved lengthwise by your butcher if possible

¼ cup dry bread crumbs

Kosher salt

Juice of 1 lemon

1 egg yolk, lightly beaten

1 bunch watercress

SERVES 2

Cut the steak into ⅓-inch-thick slices, then slice into ⅓-inch-thick strips, and then into ⅓-inch cubes. Remove the sinew, connective tissue, and fat. Refrigerate, covered, until ready to serve.

Using a small spoon, remove the raw marrow from the bone and dice it.

In a sauté pan over medium-high heat, cook the marrow meat until it's rendered into a liquid fat, about 2 minutes. Add the bread crumbs and a pinch of salt, turn the heat to low, and cook, tossing and stirring occasionally to make sure everything is evenly coated and nothing burns, until toasted, about 5 minutes. Using a slotted spoon, transfer to a bowl and let cool.

Combine the beef, bread crumbs, 2 teaspoons of the lemon juice, the egg yolk, and 2 pinches of salt in a bowl and stir well. Transfer to a serving plate and spread into a circle.

In a large bowl, toss together the watercress and the remaining lemon juice. Arrange the watercress on top of the tartare. Eat immediately.

CRAB DIP

When I lived in Winston-Salem, North Carolina, all the "nice" restaurants served crab dip. At some, it was artichoke crab dip; others specialized in spinach crab dip. When I eventually worked at one of those "nice" restaurants as a teenage waiter, I ate crab dip every day. I also drank vodka like it was a vocation. It was an addiction (crab dip and vodka) that continued for years, as I ordered it anytime I saw it on the menu. Shout out to the Village Tavern.

This is my version of that new-age faux-fancy classic; serve it with potato chips, or toast, and perhaps some freshly grated horseradish on top.

1 tablespoon unsalted butter

4 shallots, thinly sliced

1 celery rib, thinly sliced, plus a handful of celery leaves, chopped

2 cloves garlic, sliced

1 teaspoon kosher salt

7 ounces fromage blanc (from Cowgirl Creamery, if you're in California) or cream cheese

1 pound lump crabmeat (preferably Dungeness), cooked (see page 90) and picked over for shells

½ cup mayonnaise (page 216 or store-bought)

Leaves from ½ bunch flat-leaf parsley, chopped

1 tablespoon fish sauce

½ teaspoon dill seeds (optional)

¼ teaspoon celery seeds (optional)

¼ teaspoon ground white pepper

2 lemons

2 bay leaves

Freshly grated horseradish, for garnish

1 bunch chives, chopped

1 recipe potato chips (page 125)

SERVES 2 TO 4

Preheat the oven to 400°F.

Melt the butter in a skillet or sauté pan over medium heat. Add the shallots, sliced celery, garlic, and salt and cook until the vegetables are slightly wilted and the shallots are translucent, about 2 minutes.

Transfer the vegetables to a bowl, add the fromage blanc, and stir to combine. Stir in the crab meat, mayonnaise, celery leaves, parsley, fish sauce, dill seeds, celery seeds, and white pepper until well combined. Zest and juice 1 lemon and stir into the crab mixture.

Scrape the crab mixture into an ovenproof serving bowl or small baking dish. Slip in the bay leaves.

Bake until golden brown and bubbly on top and warmed through, about 20 minutes. Sprinkle with horseradish and the chives and serve with potato chips and the remaining lemon, cut into wedges. Eat immediately.

PIMENTO CHEESE

Pimento cheese is food as God intended: rich, salty, slightly sweet, slightly acidic; excellent on a burger or paired with chips, fries, or crudités; or enjoyed on its own between two slices of white bread. Try using different types of cheddar to find a personal favorite. Fresh pimentos are available at farmers' markets and specialty grocers in the summer, but the canned version is a great substitute the rest of the year.

1 teaspoon celery seeds

1 fresh or canned pimento pepper

2 egg yolks

1 teaspoon kosher salt

1 teaspoon freshly ground black pepper, plus more for garnish

1 teaspoon Urfa chile flakes or other chile flakes, plus more for garnish

½ teaspoon cayenne pepper

½ teaspoon mustard powder

1 cup neutral oil (such as safflower oil)

2 teaspoons dark molasses

1 teaspoon Worcestershire sauce

¼ cup dill pickle juice (page 64 or store-bought)

2 pounds aged sharp yellow cheddar, coarsely grated

MAKES 1 QUART

Heat a cast-iron skillet over high heat. Add the celery seeds and toast until fragrant, about 1 minute. Toss often during toasting to be sure they don't burn. Set aside to cool.

If using a fresh pimento pepper, place it over a grill or stove-top burner and cook, rotating occasionally with tongs, until blistered and charred on all sides. Quickly transfer to a covered container or a bowl with plastic wrap and let steam for 10 minutes.

Meanwhile, combine the egg yolks, toasted celery seeds, salt, black pepper, Urfa chiles, cayenne, and mustard powder in a food processor and process until combined. With the processor running, slowly add the oil and process until emulsified, about 1 minute. Add the molasses and Worcestershire and pulse to combine, then add the pickle juice and pulse to combine. Transfer to a bowl.

When the pimento is cool enough to handle, remove the charred skin and seeds and coarsely chop the pepper. If using a canned pimento pepper, drain it and then chop.

Add the chopped pepper and cheese to the bowl and mix well. Garnish with extra pepper and Urfa chile. Cover and refrigerate for up to 2 weeks. It will be ready to eat right away, but is even better if it sits overnight. Serve cold. If desired, form into a log and garnish with curly parsley. It's the next best thing to a time machine.

MUSHROOM DIP

You know what people love? Dips. Bring dips to parties. Bring dips to potluck dinners. Bring dips to bake sales. Bring dips to your couch while you watch *Bob's Burgers* reruns. Nearly any food can get dipped into a dip: Little Gem lettuce leaves, asparagus spears, french fries, potato chips, day-old bread, those curiously round little carrots, and so on and so forth. People fucking love dips. Even vegan dips, like this one.

1½ cup flaxseeds

1 cup hot water

1 tablespoon safflower oil

1 white onion, sliced

1 pound white or brown mushrooms, sliced, plus 3 or 4 sliced mushrooms for garnish

1½ teaspoons kosher salt

1 pound firm tofu, cut into small dice

5 cloves garlic, sliced

¼ cup plus 1 teaspoon sherry vinegar

1 tablespoon onion powder

1 tablespoon mushroom powder (see page 82)

Ground white pepper, to garnish

1 bunch chives, chopped

Crudités, bread, pita, or chips, for serving

SERVES 2 TO 4

In a small bowl, combine the flaxseeds and water. Stir and let soak until a puddinglike texture develops, about 5 minutes. Set aside.

Heat the oil in a large skillet or sauté pan over medium heat. Add the onion and cook, stirring occasionally, until browned and almost crispy, about 8 minutes. Add the mushrooms and ½ teaspoon of the salt, stir to combine, and cook until mushrooms are browned, about 3 minutes. Add the tofu and garlic, stir to combine, and cook until the tofu is heated through, about 3 minutes. Add the ¼ cup vinegar and deglaze the pan, using a wooden spoon to scrape up any browned bits from the bottom. Remove from the heat.

Transfer the contents of the pan to a food processor or blender and process until well incorporated and smooth and the consistency is airy and light. Add the flaxseed mixture, onion powder, mushroom powder, remaining 1 teaspoon vinegar, and remaining 1 teaspoon salt and pulse to combine.

Pour the dip into a serving bowl and sprinkle with white pepper, the chives, and remaining mushrooms. Serve immediately with crudités, bread, pita, or chips. Can be gently reheated in the oven at 300°F until warmed through.

CHICKEN WINGS SALAD

Okay, this isn't so much a salad as a bunch of fried chicken wings served in a bowl with a medley of fresh things like serrano chiles, grilled onions, cilantro, and limes. Sure beats a bucket. When serving, the chicken should still be hot from the fryer, while the "salad" is nice and cool. Encourage your eaters to eat the wings with the onions and peppers.

When it comes to frying chicken—and wings—the two-step process of brining, followed by soaking in buttermilk is my preferred route. If you have time, the best results happen when the chicken sits in each liquid for 6 to 12 hours. That said, even if you brine for an hour and then dip in buttermilk before frying, they are still going to be good—and certainly better than doing nothing at all.

3 limes

Kosher salt

2 teaspoons sugar

12 whole chicken wings (whole = drumette + wing + wing tip)

4 cups buttermilk, or as needed

1 teaspoon black peppercorns

1 teaspoon coriander seeds

1 teaspoon anise seeds

8 serrano chiles

1 red onion, halved

1 bunch cilantro, leaves and thin stems

2 cloves garlic, sliced

1 tablespoon rice vinegar

6 cups rice bran oil or other neutral oil, for frying

2 cups fine rice flour

2 tablespoons potato starch

2 tablespoons cornstarch

1 teaspoon paprika

SERVES 2 TO 4

Juice two of the limes into a small bowl. Add 1 teaspoon salt and 1 teaspoon of the sugar and stir together. Put the chicken wings in a large container, bowl, or resealable plastic bag. Pour in the lime juice mixture and turn to evenly coat the wings. Cover, refrigerate, and let the wings brine for at least 1 hour, or up to 12 hours.

Remove the chicken wings from the brine, and then, in a second large container or bowl, fully submerge them in the buttermilk. Cover, refrigerate, and let the wings soak for at least 1 hour, or up to 12 hours.

Heat a cast-iron skillet over high heat. Add the peppercorns, coriander seeds, and anise seeds and toast until fragrant, about 1 minute. Toss the spices often during toasting to be sure they don't burn. Set aside to cool. Grind using a spice grinder or mortar and pestle; set aside.

CONTINUED

Heat the skillet again over high heat. Add four of the serranos and cook, stirring occasionally, until blackened on all sides, about 6 minutes. Transfer to a large bowl.

In the same skillet, still over high heat, char the onion halves, cut side down, until blackened, 2 to 3 minutes. Slice the onion and add to the bowl with the serranos.

Thinly slice the remaining lime and add to the bowl. Add the cilantro, garlic, vinegar, 2 teaspoons salt, and the remaining 1 teaspoon sugar and stir to combine. Set aside.

In a Dutch oven or heavy pot, heat the oil over high heat to 385°F, making sure you have 3 inches of oil.

While the oil is heating, combine the rice flour, potato starch, cornstarch, paprika, and a pinch of salt in a large bowl. Working with one chicken wing at a time, remove it from the buttermilk, then dredge it in the flour mixture, turning it to evenly coat.

When the oil hits 385°F, fry the wings until golden brown and cooked through, about 5 minutes, working in batches to make sure the wings don't touch each other. Adjust the heat as needed to maintain the oil temperature at 365°F. Using a spider skimmer or other small strainer, remove the wings from the oil and drain on paper towels. Sprinkle them with the spice mixture. Slice the remaining four serrano peppers into coins and add to the bowl with the vegetables. Add the fried wings to the bowl and toss well to combine. Arrange on a large platter or in a large bowl as an entire "salad." Eat immediately.

A COOL RECIPE FOR HOT CHICKEN

This recipe is pretty darn cool and the chicken is pretty darn hot. Nothing is mild.

12 whole chicken wings (whole = drumette + wing + wing tip)

3 cups dill pickle juice (page 64 or store-bought); enough to submerge the wings

3 cups buttermilk, if brining, or enough to submerge all the wings (see Note)

2 tablespoons plus 1 teaspoon paprika

2 tablespoons onion powder

1 tablespoon garlic powder

1 tablespoon mustard powder

1 tablespoon cayenne pepper

½ tablespoon freshly ground black pepper

1 tablespoon brown sugar

1½ teaspoons plus 1 pinch of kosher salt

1 teaspoon ground white pepper

½ teaspoon mace

½ cup unsalted butter

6 cups rice bran oil or other neutral oil, for frying

2 cups fine rice flour

2 tablespoons potato starch

2 tablespoons cornstarch

Sliced white bread, for serving

Bread and butter pickle slices (page 223 or store-bought), for serving

SERVES 2 TO 4

Put the chicken wings in a large container, bowl, or resealable plastic bag. Pour in the pickle juice and evenly coat the wings. Cover, refrigerate, and let the wings brine for at least 1 hour, or up to 12 hours.

Remove the wings from the brine. In a second large container or bowl, fully submerge them in the buttermilk. Cover, refrigerate, and let the wings soak for at least 1 hour, or up to 12 hours.

In a large bowl, stir together 2 tablespoons of the paprika, onion powder, garlic powder, mustard powder, cayenne, black pepper, brown sugar, 1½ teaspoons of the salt, white pepper, and mace.

Melt the butter in a large skillet or frying pan over high heat and continue to cook until it browns a little around the edges and you smell the nutty fragrance of brown butter. Add the spice mixture and immediately turn off the heat. Stir until well combined. Return the spices to the bowl.

In a Dutch oven or heavy pot, heat the oil over high heat to 385°F, making sure you have 3 inches of oil.

While the oil is heating, combine the rice flour, potato starch, cornstarch, remaining 1 teaspoon paprika, and a pinch of salt in a large bowl. Working with one chicken wing at a time, remove it from the buttermilk, then dredge it in the flour mixture, turning it to evenly coat.

When the oil hits 385°F, fry the wings until golden brown and cooked through, about 5 minutes, working in two batches to make sure the wings don't touch each other. Adjust the heat as needed to maintain the oil temperature at 365°F. Using a spider skimmer or other small strainer, remove the wings from the oil and drain on paper towels. While the wings drain, add ½ cup of the hot oil to the spice mixture to combine. Transfer the wings to the bowl with the spice mixture and toss well to evenly coat. Serve atop sliced white bread alongside pickles. Eat immediately.

Note: If not brining, you just need enough buttermilk to coat all the wings, 2 cups or so.

GRILLED CHICKEN WINGS

If you already have a fire for burgers, make the most of it and cook more than just one thing. Use the grill for other courses, like chicken wings for appetizers and grilled vegetables for sides. These chicken wings are a particularly fine candidate for a barbecue addition because nearly all the work is done before cooking, allowing you—master of the grill, burger whisperer, and envy of all your guests—to simply grill them up and serve.

12 whole chicken wings (whole = drumette + wing + wing tip)

1 orange, thinly sliced

2 lemons; 1 thinly sliced, 1 halved

1 bunch spring onions, trimmed

1 teaspoon kosher salt

1 teaspoon sugar

1 teaspoon cumin seeds

1 tablespoon Szechuan peppercorns, crushed

1 teaspoon black peppercorns

1 tablespoon honey

SERVES 2 TO 4

Put the chicken wings in a large container, bowl, or resealable plastic bag. Add the orange, sliced lemon, spring onions, salt, and sugar and turn everything until evenly coated. Cover, refrigerate, and let the wings brine at least 12 hours or up to overnight.

Heat a cast-iron skillet over high heat. Add the cumin seeds, Szechuan peppercorns, and black peppercorns and toast until fragrant, about 1 minute. Toss the spices often during toasting to be sure they don't burn. Remove from the heat. Grind using a spice grinder or mortar and pestle; set aside.

Heat a grill over medium heat. Transfer the entire chicken mixture, onions and citrus included, to the grill. Spread evenly and grill everything until the wings are cooked through, 10 to 15 minutes. Make sure to flip them and get char on both sides. Remove from the heat and set on a platter.

Drizzle the wings with honey and sprinkle evenly with the spice mixture. Serve with the lemon halves and apply juice as desired

GRILLED VEGETABLES

The transformative power of cooking with fire is truly a wonder to behold. I'm constantly in awe of a flame's ability to positively affect anything, turning a simple ingredient like a spring onion or potato or squash into something beyond, with just the addition of a little salt and acid. A burger is delicious. Imparting that extra bit of flavor through a wood fire is a very simple action that can take it to a whole different place. That idea translates to anything, including—drum roll, please—vegetables.

When grilling vegetables, simplicity is best. Wash your vegetable, or vegetables, of choice. Keep them whole, or cut them in half. There's no wrong answer. Put the vegetables directly on a clean grill over coals, so they cook over medium-high heat, but not directly over live flames. How long should you cook your vegetables? As long as you want. If you like them closer to raw, do that. If you like them more caramelized and wilted, do that. Sprinkle with salt and lemon juice. If you're getting really fancy, serve with aioli (page 219).

Burger Sides

PADRÓNS

Think of this recipe more as a template than a true instructional procedure. Padrón peppers, and similar small summer peppers like shishito and gypsy, make great appetizers during their season. And you don't need to do much to them. The point is that you just need the core components—peppers, heat, chile flakes, and cheese. The specific cheese doesn't matter; its savory tartness does. The chile flakes don't either—their spicy kick does. Not even the heat source is super important, as long as you can get the peppers nice and blistered. Toss them in a cast-iron skillet and place it on the stove, on the grill, under a broiler, in a pizza oven, on the engine block of your car. Ladies and gentlemen, anything is possible.

1½ pounds Padrón peppers

1 tablespoon neutral oil (such as safflower oil)

Kosher salt

Splash of sherry vinegar

1 tablespoon honey

Chile flakes (Urfa, Aleppo, and Marash are my favorites), for sprinkling

Hard, salty cheese (dry Jack, pecorino, Parmigiano-Reggiano, and cotija are my favorites), for grating

SERVES 2 TO 4

In a bowl, toss the peppers with the oil until well coated.

In a cast-iron skillet, heat the peppers over medium-high heat and cook until browned, 4 to 5 minutes. Once slightly blistered, toss in a large bowl with a pinch of salt. Add the vinegar and honey and mix well. Transfer to a serving platter, or if you're going for that whole rustic and holistic thing, back into the cast-iron skillet. Sprinkle with a generous amount of chile flakes, as much as you like, and then grate cheese over the peppers. Eat immediately.

CHAPTER
5

WEDGE SALAD

Dating back to the early twentieth century, the wedge salad is about as American as any salad gets. It's also one of my favorites, so it's fitting that it's been on our menu since day one.

A great wedge salad starts with crunchy iceberg lettuce. Accept no substitutes. Iceberg has been maligned in recent years, so often an object of derision in this post-kale era. I love herbs in salads, and the addition of fines herbes—a core element of traditional French cooking—lends the dish just enough sophistication to give it an edge over any tired steak-house or country-club version.

But the dish really relies on the assertive blue cheese dressing, a balanced concoction that's both acidic and salty. If you can, opt for a raw-milk blue cheese from Point Reyes Station, a small bucolic community about an hour north of San Francisco. The Point Reyes Farmstead Cheese Company, established in 1904, makes some beautiful blue cheeses from its small herd of cows. It's a cheese that can't be made anywhere but in Northern California. It's so good that, in addition to mixing a hearty portion of it into the dressing, I like to crumble more of it over the salad.

This recipe will yield a large batch of dressing. Use leftovers as a dip with chicken wings (page 140) or your favorite raw vegetables.

BLUE CHEESE DRESSING

¼ teaspoon celery seeds

¼ cup red wine vinegar

1 egg yolk

¾ teaspoon kosher salt

1 small clove garlic, chopped

½ teaspoon ground fennel seeds

¼ teaspoon mustard powder

¼ teaspoon freshly ground black pepper

¾ cup vegetable oil

¼ white onion, coarsely chopped

¼ bunch tarragon, leaves and thin stems

¼ bunch dill, leaves and thin stems

¼ bunch flat-leaf parsley, leaves and thin stems

1½ teaspoons Worcestershire sauce

½ cup crème fraîche

3 ounces crumbled blue cheese (preferably Point Reyes Original Blue)

SALAD

4 ounces bacon (preferably slab bacon), cut into 1 by ¼-inch lardons or strips

1 head iceberg lettuce, cored and cut into 4 wedges

4 ounces crumbled blue cheese (preferably Point Reyes Original Blue)

½ bunch tarragon, leaves and thin stems

½ bunch dill, leaves and thin stems

½ bunch flat-leaf parsley, leaves and thin stems

1 bunch chives, cut into 1-inch segments

1 bunch chervil, leaves and thin stems

1 cup halved cherry tomatoes or chopped tomato

3 to 4 breakfast radishes or 1 to 2 watermelon radishes, thinly sliced

Kosher salt

Juice of 1 lemon

Freshly ground black pepper

SERVES 2 TO 4

CONTINUED

To make the dressing: Heat a cast-iron skillet over high heat. Add the celery seeds and toast until fragrant, about 1 minute. Toss often during toasting to be sure they don't burn. Remove from the heat and set aside.

Combine ¼ cup of the vinegar, the egg yolks, salt, garlic, fennel, mustard powder, pepper, and toasted celery seeds in a food processor and pulse to combine. With the processor running, slowly pour in ½ cup of the oil. Stop the processor; add the onion, tarragon, dill, and parsley; and pulse again until smooth and well incorporated, scraping down the sides of the food processor if necessary. With the processor running, slowly add another ½ cup of the oil. Add the remaining ¼ cup of the vinegar and pulse to incorporate. With the processor running, add the remaining ½ cup of the oil and process until emulsified, about 30 seconds.

Add the Worcestershire, crème fraîche, and blue cheese to the processor and give a quick whir until they are well combined. Do not overprocess. Pour the dressing into a bowl, cover, and refrigerate for up to 2 weeks. The dressing is ready to use right away, but will be even better if a little bit cold.

To make the salad: Heat a skillet over medium-high heat. Add the bacon and cook until brown with a crispy exterior and soft interior, about 5 minutes. Remove from the heat and drain on paper towels. Let cool.

On a large platter, arrange the iceberg wedges. Dress generously by pouring the blue cheese dressing on top of the wedges. The amount is up to you, but I prefer ½ cup per wedge, with more on the side. Sprinkle with the crumbled blue cheese and bacon.

In a large bowl, toss together the tarragon, dill, parsley, chives, chervil, tomatoes, and radishes. Add a pinch of salt and the lemon juice and toss again. Put the herb salad atop the iceberg wedges. Finish with freshly ground black pepper. Eat immediately.

GRILLED CABBAGE WITH GRAPEFRUIT

Grilled salads—what a world. Giving charred, burned, or smoked flavors to a salad is one of my favorite tricks (you'll see it in a couple of other recipes, too). It's a small thing, and often one that takes only a few minutes, especially if you've already got a grill going. But it can make a huge difference in a salad—it adds a little more complexity, a little more texture, a little more primal fire-kissed goodness. In other words: You're grilling burgers already. Char some cabbage while you're at it.

We do two versions of this cabbage salad; both have the same method but the ingredients change slightly. One is an all-white rendition, anchored by the white Marsh grapefruit that grows in Central California during the late winter and early spring months. It gets paired with light green cabbage and white sesame seeds. This is the other version, made with red cabbage, red grapefruit, black sesame seeds, and a kumquat-sesame dressing. (Using whole kumquats is what makes this dressing. But if you can't find kumquats, substitute the rind of 1 orange and its juice.)

Pro Tip No. 1: Put a piece of fried chicken on it. Voilà, now you have the best chicken salad ever. Pro Tip No. 2: Put a piece of fried chicken on anything.

DRESSING
¼ cup sesame oil
¼ cup tahini
15 to 20 (about 8 ounces) kumquats
½ teaspoon kosher salt
2 tablespoons cider vinegar

SALAD
1 head red cabbage, cut into 8 wedges
2 Ruby Red grapefruits
Juice of ½ lemon
Kosher salt
1 bunch chives, chopped
2 tablespoons toasted black sesame seeds

SERVES 2 TO 4

To make the dressing: Combine the sesame oil, tahini, kumquats, salt, and vinegar in a blender and process until smooth. Set aside.

To make the salad: In a heavy frying pan or on a grill over high heat, cook the cabbage just long enough to char its exterior, 2 to 3 minutes on each side. Remove from the heat. When cool enough to handle, cut each wedge horizontally into bite-size pieces, 1 to 2 inches each. Transfer to a large bowl.

Cut the grapefruits into supremes or wedges. To supreme the citrus, cut off the rind and pith, essentially revealing the fruit inside. Following the membrane of each individual segment as closely as possible, make two slices in each segment; the wedge of fruit should pop out, leaving the membrane attached.

When ready to serve, add the lemon juice to the cabbage and toss to coat. Add ½ cup of the sesame dressing and a generous sprinkle of salt and toss again. Arrange the cabbage on a platter and top with the grapefruits, chives, and sesame seeds. Eat immediately.

TOMATO AND OYSTER SALAD

There is an art to making a salad. This isn't to say that some salads cannot be casually tossed together, but others do require a bit more care. This is particularly true when using delicate ingredients, like oysters and tomatoes.

2 baby leeks, white and green parts, sliced

1 shallot, minced

Kosher salt

1 tablespoon champagne vinegar

12 bright briny oysters (such as Miyagi)

½ cup dry vermouth

¼ cup neutral oil (such as safflower oil)

1½ pounds heirloom tomatoes, cut into bite-size pieces

1 lemon, halved

1 cucumber (preferably Armenian), sliced

Handful of fennel fronds, for garnish (optional)

Handful of purslane and fresh summer herbs, for garnish

Freshly ground black pepper

SERVES 2 TO 4

Soak the sliced leeks in a bowl of ice water. After about 10 minutes, drain and let dry on paper towels.

Combine the shallot and a pinch of salt in a bowl and let sit for 2 minutes. Add the vinegar and let sit while you proceed with the rest of the recipe.

Shuck the oysters, making sure to save the oyster liquid. Put both the oyster meat and its liqueur into a bowl.

Heat the vermouth in a small saucepan over high heat until it's just about to simmer, then immediately remove from the heat. Working quickly and using a slotted spoon, drop the oysters—but not their liqueur, which you should keep in the bowl—into the vermouth. Poach the oysters ever so slightly,

about 15 seconds each, before transferring them to a cutting board. Repeat with the other oysters, then let the oysters cool. Don't toss the vermouth cooking liquid; let it cool.

When the oysters are cool, quarter them and add to the bowl with the shallot and vinegar. Pour the oyster liquid through a fine-mesh strainer or cheesecloth into the bowl. Add the oil, 2 tablespoons of the vermouth cooking liquid, and ¼ teaspoon salt. Stir to combine and set aside.

Put the tomatoes in a large bowl. Add the juice of a lemon half and a generous pinch of salt. Using your hands, gently toss it once, starting from the bottom and moving the bottom tomatoes to the top. Make sure everything is evenly coated. Remove the tomatoes gently, leaving the juices behind, and spread evenly on a serving platter. This is an important step because you don't want your salad to turn into a tomato soup. Discard the tomato juice.

Put the cucumber in the now-empty bowl. Add the juice of the remaining lemon half and a generous pinch of salt. Gently toss the cucumber, making sure everything is evenly coated. Add the cucumbers to the serving platter.

Just before serving, toss the leeks with a pinch of salt and a squeeze of lemon in a small bowl.

Spoon the oyster vinaigrette over the salad. Scatter with the leeks, fennel fronds, and summer herbs and grind black pepper over the top. Eat immediately.

A PERFECTLY SIMPLE CHICORY SALAD

Perhaps more than any other type of lettuce, a perfectly dressed leaf of chicory can be magical. Sometimes you just want a simple salad, without a million components; no clutter, just a burst of crunchy, tart bitterness. The chicory can stand up to a dressing with some punch. Besides, there's something special about knowing how to craft a simple salad, with a deceptively interesting dressing.

½ cup neutral oil (such as safflower oil)

4 cloves garlic, sliced

¼ cup champagne vinegar

¼ cup pomegranate molasses

1 tablespoon honey

1 (2-inch) piece ginger, peeled and grated

2 teaspoons kosher salt

1 head escarole

1 head Castelfranco radicchio

1 head Treviso radicchio

12 to 18 dates, pitted

Leaves from 1 bunch mint

SERVES 4

Heat the oil in a small saucepan over medium-high heat. Once the temperature reaches 260°F, add the garlic and turn off the heat. You don't want to fry the garlic, just sweat them, so their flavors mellow and open up a little. Remove from the heat and transfer to a large bowl. Let the oil and garlic cool.

When the garlic oil is cool, add the vinegar, pomegranate molasses, honey, ginger, and salt and stir to combine. Set this dressing aside.

Wash the chicories and then segment into bite-size pieces. For the escarole and Castelfranco, tear the leaves; for the Treviso, cut the leaves on the bias, splitting them. Toss to combine in a large bowl. Add the dates and the dressing. Using salad tongs or your hands, mix gently, but thoroughly. The chicories are hearty, so you can handle them a little more than normal lettuce. Taste for seasoning. Sprinkle the mint in last. Eat immediately.

About Oil

Sharp-eyed readers might notice that many of these salad recipes call for neutral oil.

Neutral oils allow other flavors to shine, while still providing the textural and structural benefit of oil. Olive oil and sesame oil are not neutral oils; they have distinct flavors. As such, I like using them when their respective flavors actually complement the accompanying ingredients, like in the case of olive oil in tuna salad (page 168) or sesame oil in cabbage salad (page 153).

Particularly when the ingredients are distinctive, like tomatoes and oysters, or blue cheese dressing, neutral oils are the best options. Generally speaking, the best option for neutral oils is an organic safflower or sunflower oil, but the more common canola or vegetable oils also work. Choose organic if you can.

VEGAN CHOPPED SALAD

We had the Wedge Salad (page 150). We needed a vegan equivalent. I tasked the very talented William Niles and Christa Chase, the opening chefs of Kronnerburger, with the challenge. We wanted satisfying, big flavors in a salad with classic roots. Despite the vegan angle, it still had to be hearty. A chopped salad turned out to be a natural fit. Along with the wedge and the Caesar, it's the "other" steak-house salad and is usually made with some combination of bite-size portions of lettuce, chicken breast, cured meat, tomatoes, garbanzo beans, a cheese of some sort, and whatever else the kitchen might have on hand. The greatness of a classic chopped salad is the way the various components intermingle; it's less about the actual ingredients than the variety of textures and flavors: crunch, acid, sweetness, heat.

This is a vegan version of that salad but it checks those same textural boxes and it shines because of the combination of techniques: pickling, smoking, charring. In that sense, this isn't so much a recipe as a template. Once you have the framework—something leafy, something charred, something acidic, something crunchy, something spicy, something sweet, something seedy—you can mix and match whatever you like to eat. If tomatoes are in season, use them. For the crunchy components, toss in chunks of apples and paper-thin slices of beets or radishes, or various bite-size raw pieces of squash, Romano beans, and carrots. In the summer, add whole blackberries and wedges of plums. You can even give it a hippie twist by garnishing it with seeds (sesame, chia) or nuts or even a hacky sack.

1 spring onion, halved lengthwise [something charred]

Kosher salt

12 or so green beans, cut into 1-inch segments

1 ear corn, kernels cut off from cob [something sweet]

1 head hearty greens (such as radicchio or romaine) [something leafy]

1 apple, sliced thinly [something crunchy]

Juice of ½ lemon [something acidic]

¾ cup smoked coconut dressing (recipe follows)

½ cup Quick Pickled Chiles (page 223), or more if desired [something spicy]

1 beet, peeled and sliced thinly with a vegetable peeler [another something crunchy]

½ cup seeds or nuts (such as peanuts, cashews, or toasted flaxseeds) [something seedy]

SERVES 2 TO 4

In a cast-iron pan or on a grill over high heat, place the spring onion halves cut side down and cook until deeply caramelized, 3 to 4 minutes. Remove from the heat and let cool. When cool enough to handle, cut into bite-size pieces.

Bring a pot of water to a boil over high heat and add enough salt so that the water tastes like the sea. Prepare a salty ice bath.

Gently add the green beans to the boiling water and cook until just barely tender, about 30 seconds. Using a small strainer, quickly transfer to the ice bath and let cool completely. Drain in a colander and let dry on paper towels.

Combine the spring onion, green beans, corn, greens, and apple in a large bowl. Add the lemon juice, 2 pinches of salt, and the dressing and toss until everything is well coated.

Arrange the salad on your serving platter, or plates, and scatter the pickled chiles, beets, and seeds on top. Eat immediately.

SMOKED COCONUT DRESSING

This smoky coconut dressing is a workhorse in the restaurant due to its versatility and vegan nature. The smoky sweetness adds an entirely new dimension—a meaty one, despite being vegan. It is definitely the most time-intensive dressing in this book, requiring making a vegan mayo and then smoking the coconut cream and flakes (see "Smoking Your Food in a Home Kitchen" on page 163). Sorry about that. But like most things in life, the extra effort is rewarding. The dressing keeps for weeks and can be eaten on its own with raw or roasted vegetables, making for an even simpler serving option.

½ cup coconut cream

½ cup toasted unsweetened coconut flakes

¼ cup coconut oil, melted

¼ cup Tofu Mayo (page 218) or store-bought vegan mayonnaise

2 tablespoons cider vinegar

½ teaspoon kosher salt

MAKES ¾ CUP

Select two small metal or glass bowls that can simultaneously fit in your smoking contraption, which will either be a large pot with a tight-fitting lid or a stove-top smoker. Put the coconut cream in one bowl and the coconut flakes in the other. Put both bowls, uncovered, in the smoking contraption. Add hot embers (wood, not charcoal) or smoking chips and smoke for 5 minutes. Remove from the smoker.

Combine the smoked coconut cream, smoked coconut flakes, coconut oil, mayo, vinegar, and salt in a blender and process until smooth. Transfer to an airtight container and store in the refrigerator for up to 3 weeks.

Burger Noir

By Anna Dunn, co-author of *Dinner at the Long Table*

Any good detective would tell you to never judge a book by its cover. But of course that's the first thing the rest of us naturally do. And if you were to judge this book by its cover you would believe it to be a masterful meditation on the classic Americana food: the burger. And you wouldn't be wrong. *Burger for president! Burgers in the streets!*

Us mortals, we like it linear, cover to cover, left to right, bottom to top, between two buns. We like it medium rare, with onion and tomato. We like it juicy, broiled. We like it satisfying and we like it bloody. But a detective might start closer to the center of something.

If we were to start at the center, to stare deep into the leafy heart of Chris Kronner what I suspect we might find is the shape of a head of lettuce, crisp and crunchy, and spiked with herbs, its inner ethereal chamber maybe red with the ache of heirloom tomato or sentimental as a sluice of caper aioli.

One afternoon, a hot one, I stood in the street at the intersection of Green and West, the farthest north corner of Brooklyn. Lee Desrosier's nightly fire blazed in the empty lot behind Achilles Heel. I was in a bad mood. Regardless, I was the food runner. The delivery system. On a double. And Chris Kronner was on deck, slinging burgers off the wood-fired grill.

The corner was mobbed. Friends. Families. Foes. Children. Dogs. Trannies. DJs. Dancers. Lovers. Chefs. Bats. Cats. Detectives. All were present. I must have run approximately one zillion burgers that night, and I mean running, ducking, dodging, leaping over tow-headed toddlers to deliver burger after burger to hungry, sweating, adoring Kronnerburger fans. However, what struck me was, alongside every burger order, there were two and sometimes three salad orders accompanying it. Little boats of emerald jewels. Bibb lettuce. Breakfast radish. Scallion. Basil. Razor clam.

As the sun went down, dropping gold all along the river, I looked around my city and thought about how burgers are good food for the weary. But salad . . . salad is how you seduce someone, and a good detective never sleeps.

SMOKING YOUR FOOD IN A HOME KITCHEN

Don't be afraid to smoke ingredients at home. I'm not talking about spending hours and hours tending to meats in a special outdoor smoker, but rather, quick-smoking ingredients for added flavor. It's more of a seasoning technique than a cooking method, and it's a handy way to add extra heartiness to vegan and vegetarian dishes.

Smoking vegetables, even for a few minutes, is one of the best tricks to add to your culinary arsenal. Smoked Coconut Dressing (page 159) shines thanks to a few quick minutes of smoke, easily created on your grill or even on your stove top.

Options abound for smoking at home.

If you've got a wood fire going in your grill (I like using oak wood, but almond wood or really any fruitwood works well), find a smoking ember about the size of a baseball. You don't want an ember that's aflame, just smoldering, but still very clearly a piece of wood, as opposed to a spent briquette. Remove it from the pit or grill and put it in a large heavy pot (or metal pan large enough to allow space between what you are smoking and the wood) with a tight-fitting lid. Add the ingredients you want to smoke to the pot and cover it. Let the ember smoke inside the pot until it is cashed out, about 5 minutes. (One thing to note: Don't use charcoal for smoking. Wood, and the flavor it brings, is key.)

If you do not have a wood fire going, you can easily use your stove top and wood chips. There are some great stainless-steel stove-top smokers available for less than fifty dollars, or you can use a pot with a tight-fitting lid. Wrap the wood chips in an aluminum foil packet (or as instructed by the manufacturer). Place it in the stove-top smoker over the burner and heat until smoking. Add the ingredients you want to smoke to the smoker or pot and cover it. Let smoke until there's a distinctly smoky flavor; the time it takes to absorb the flavor varies depending on the density of the ingredient. Taste to check the intensity of the smoky flavor; for a stronger flavor, leave it in longer. For dressing and sauces, you'll need only a few minutes for the flavor to infuse, but for dense vegetables like cooked potatoes or carrots, it will take longer. The little bit nuance—that hint of char—that a few minutes of smoke can add to a salad or side, however, is worth it.

OKRA AND MUSHROOM SALAD

Though I had eaten okra while growing up in North Carolina, it wasn't until I went to Japan that I encountered okra served raw. There, it had been combined with *natto*, a fermented soybean, in an unexpectedly delicious salad. It was about as far removed as possible from the fried okra coins and Texas Pete hot sauce served in my high school cafeteria. The okra, raw and thinly sliced, was a revelation, like a raw chile salad without the heat and better texture. I was taken. For this salad, we lose the Japanese fermented soybeans and create a light, bright, and satisfying salad that provides a perfect showcase of the wonderful summer ingredient that is okra.

½ cup sunflower seeds

4 teaspoons sunflower oil or other neutral oil

8 ounces maitake mushrooms, separated

Kosher salt

1 tablespoon freshly squeezed lemon juice, or to taste

1 tablespoon sherry vinegar

10 ounces (about 20 pieces) fresh okra, cut on the diagonal into ¼-inch slices

Handful of sunflower sprouts

Grated dry Jack or aged cheddar cheese, for garnish

SERVES 2

Heat a cast-iron skillet over medium-high heat. Add the sunflower seeds and toast until fragrant, 3 to 4 minutes. Toss the seeds often during toasting to be sure they don't burn. Remove from the heat and set aside.

Heat 1 teaspoon of the oil in a sauté pan over high heat. Add the mushrooms and a pinch of salt and cook until the mushrooms are heated through and take on just a little bit of color, 2 to 3 minutes. Don't cook them too much; you want some texture and bounce. Remove from the heat and let cool.

Combine 2 teaspoons of the oil, the lemon juice, vinegar, and ½ teaspoon salt in a large bowl. Whisk together. Add the okra, cooked mushrooms, and sunflower sprouts and toss until everything is well coated. Arrange the salad on a serving platter.

Combine the toasted sunflower seeds, the remaining 1 teaspoon of oil, and a pinch of salt in a small bowl and toss until evenly coated. Scatter the seeds and cheese over the top of the salad. Eat immediately.

RADISH AND STONE FRUIT CAESAR SALAD

We've got a wedge salad. We've got a chopped salad. The final member of the triumvirate of archetypal steak-house salads is the Caesar salad.

Apologies to the romaine and crouton enthusiasts out there, but the thing that truly defines a Caesar is its dressing: cheesy, fishy, creamy, sharp. But there's a plot twist! What happens if you make a Caesar dressing with neither eggs nor oil? Let's find out.

This version, made with relatively firm but ripe stone fruit (apricots, plums, peaches, nectarines, and so on), is the one we do in the summer, but the dressing miraculously works anywhere you'd usually traditionally use Caesar dressing, even on romaine.

12 assorted small radishes, sliced

Juice of ½ lemon

Kosher salt

⅓ cup plus 1 teaspoon dressing (recipe follows)

1 apricot, pitted and sliced

1 nectarine, pitted and cut into bite-size chunks

1 peach, pitted and cut into bite-size chunks

2 small plums, pitted and sliced

⅓ cup chopped roasted pistachios

Pecorino Romano cheese, for grating

SERVES 2

Combine the radishes, lemon juice, and a few pinches of salt in a small bowl and toss together. Add ⅓ cup of the dressing and toss gently and thoroughly again. Place the dressed radishes on a serving platter.

Put the apricot, nectarine, peach, and plums in the same bowl and add 1 teaspoon dressing and a tiny pinch of salt. (The stone fruits don't require as much dressing as the radishes, so they should be dressed separately.) Place the stone fruits atop the radishes on the platter. Sprinkle with the pistachios and grate the Pecorino Romano over the top. Eat immediately.

DRESSING

3 ounces Pecorino Romano cheese, broken into chunks

½ cup red wine vinegar

4 salted anchovy fillets, rinsed

2 small cloves garlic, crushed with the side of your knife

½ teaspoon kosher salt

½ teaspoon nigella seeds

⅛ teaspoon celery seeds

MAKES ½ CUP

Combine all the ingredients in a high-speed blender or food processor and process until smooth. This recipe will make slightly more than you need for this salad, but you can use the dressing for nearly any salad. And since there are no eggs, it can keep longer. Cover and store in the refrigerator for up to 1 week.

TUNA SALAD

During the twentieth century, America embraced mayonnaise-heavy salads, gloppy hodgepodges of celery and salt that got packed into containers for family picnics and religious gatherings. Flip open any midcentury cookbook and you'll find a medley of (often cringe-worthy) mayo- or gelatin-based "salads." Of those, a handful—namely, chicken, potato, and tuna salads—have persevered. These salads are picnic stalwarts.

This version of tuna salad upends the gloppy tradition and instead embraces a fresher turn, full of summer vegetables. Instead of mayo, the primary binding agent is an eggplant puree. And because it's a summer dish, fresh green herbs and juicy cherry tomatoes are tossed into the mix, too. All the components can be prepared ahead of time and assembled on the eating day.

Rather than using canned tuna, we make our own version of tuna confit, which is great in this salad or anywhere you would normally use canned tuna. We pour hot, herbaceous oil over raw cubes of tuna and then let the entire mixture cool to room temperature. The effect is the canned tuna of your dreams, except the fish isn't cooked to death or stripped of all flavor. Instead, it is aggressively seasoned and barely cooked—just like a rare burger.

If you prefer the tuna fully cooked, as opposed to medium-rare, cut the cubes into ¼-inch chunks. Also note that the eggplant puree is great as a sandwich spread or dip.

DELICIOUS TUNA CONFIT

8 ounces quality albacore or yellowtail tuna, cut into ½-inch chunks

1 teaspoon kosher salt

Juice of ½ lemon

1 teaspoon coriander seeds

1 teaspoon fennel seeds

1 star anise pod

1¼ cups extra-virgin olive oil

1 tablespoon Urfa, Marash, or Aleppo chile flakes

4 cloves garlic, sliced

FISHOLI

Juice of ½ lemon

1 egg yolk

1 clove garlic, sliced

1 pinch of kosher salt

1 cup of the tuna oil from the tuna confit

CHARRED EGGPLANT PUREE

2 small (about 8 ounces each) eggplants

2 tablespoons sherry vinegar

1 tablespoon pomegranate molasses

1 clove garlic

1 teaspoon salt

2 tablespoons extra-virgin olive oil

Kosher salt

8 ounces cherry tomatoes (preferably Sun Gold)

½ lemon

1 bunch watercress, thick stems removed

SERVES 2

To make the tuna confit: Put the tuna in a heat-proof container, such as a bowl or small baking dish. Sprinkle with the salt and lemon juice.

Heat a small pot over medium-high heat. Add the coriander seeds, fennel seeds, and star anise and toast until fragrant, 15 to 20 seconds. Toss or stir the spices during toasting to be sure they don't burn. Using a spice grinder or mortar and pestle, grind the spices and return to the pot.

Add the oil to the pot and heat over medium-high heat until the oil reaches 250°F and the spices have started to fry, about 1 minute. Add the chile flakes and garlic, and then immediately turn off the heat. Let the oil steep for about 2 minutes. Pour the infused oil over the tuna. Shake it gently in the dish to make sure the tuna is completely covered. Let sit until it reaches room temperature, about 30 minutes. The exterior should be fully cooked, but inside, the flesh should be firm but rare. Cut a piece and check for doneness.

Once cooled, use the tuna immediately or refrigerate, covered, in the oil overnight. When ready to use, remove the tuna from the oil, reserving the oil for the fishy aioli (fisholi).

To make the fisholi: Combine the lemon juice, egg yolk, garlic, and salt in a food processor and process until combined. With the processor running, slowly add the oil and process until emulsified, about 30 seconds. Transfer to an airtight container and store in the refrigerator for up to 2 days.

To make the eggplant puree: If you can, use a live fire to char one of the eggplants on all sides over high heat until evenly blackened and soft, about 2 minutes per side. If you don't have a grill, set the eggplant directly on the burner.

Immediately put the charred eggplant in a sealed container, like a Tupperware or small pot. Cover and let it steam for about 10 minutes. This step will make it easier to peel. When mostly cooled, peel off the majority of the skin—about 80 percent. It's okay if you don't get it all; you want to keep some of it for its smoky flavor.

Combine the eggplant, vinegar, pomegranate molasses, garlic, and salt in a blender and process until smooth. Transfer to a bowl and set aside.

Peel the remaining eggplant and cut into 1-inch cubes. Heat 1 tablespoon of the oil in a large sauté pan over medium-high heat. Add the eggplant cubes and a pinch of salt and cook until the skin is browned and the eggplant is just cooked through, about 3 minutes. Transfer to a large bowl and set aside.

Heat the remaining 1 tablespoon of the oil in the same pan over medium-high heat. Add the tomatoes and a pinch of salt and immediately shake the pan, gently tossing the tomatoes until they're evenly coated. Then let the tomatoes cook, undisturbed, until blistered on one side. When they start to split, about 3 minutes, transfer to a bowl. Add a pinch of salt, gently toss, and add to the eggplant, followed by a squirt of lemon juice. Toss to coat.

For a fancy presentation: Spread the eggplant puree on a large serving platter. Arrange the tomato and eggplant mixture on top of the puree. Add the tuna. Give the watercress a thorough squirt of lemon juice, toss to coat, and scatter the watercress leaves over the top. Finally, drizzle the fisholi over the top.

For a picnic, in a bowl: Combine the tomato-eggplant mixture, puree, tuna, watercress, and lemon juice and toss well. Drizzle with fisholi. Or make a sandwich.

LOUIE SALAD
(AKA SEA SALAD)

When I make this updated version of a crab Louie salad, I always put as much seafood on it as I can—crab, shrimp, prawns, lobster. But then again, I will also buy three pounds of king crab legs and eat them all by myself because I'm a disgusting person and I cannot control my love for consuming shellfish and crustaceans. Here's how I rationalize it: While so much of our seafood is in peril, most shellfish and crustaceans are very sustainable. The way I see it, crustaceans will probably inherit the seas. One day in a not-too-distant dystopian future, humankind will be down at the beaches shooting giant crabs to prevent them from coming onto the shore to take our bitcoin, because they—and their jellyfish overlords—will be the only things left in the ocean. They might be the kings of the sea but they won't be the kings of the beach, as long as us humans and our Amazon delivery drone allies have anything to do with it. So basically, that's why I eat as much crab as I can these days—to prevent a crab ground war.

This salad serves as a hearty shared starter or stand-alone entrée. If you want to skip the salad, just use the dressing—or its leftovers—in a seafood cocktail, with shrimp, crab, lobster tails, whatever.

DRESSING

12 Jimmy Nardello peppers, or 2 red bell peppers (about 8 ounces total)

1 cup plus 2 tablespoons neutral oil (such as safflower oil)

Kosher salt

2 egg yolks

2 cloves garlic, chopped

2 tablespoons cider vinegar

1 teaspoon mustard powder

¼ cup crème fraîche

2 tablespoons ketchup (preferably Sir Kensington's)

1 tablespoon Worcestershire sauce

1 teaspoon Tabasco or other fermented hot sauce

½ shallot, minced

¼ cup diced dill pickles (page 64 or store-bought)

SALAD

Kosher salt

1 pound shrimp or prawns, peeled and deveined

2 small heads iceberg lettuce, or 4 heads Little Gem lettuce, cored and chopped into bite-size pieces

½ lemon

1 pound Dungeness crab (about 1 crab), cooked (see page 90) and picked over for shells

4 semi-soft-boiled eggs (see page 173), peeled and halved

Fresh dill leaves, for garnish

SERVES 2 TO 4

CONTINUED

To make the dressing: Preheat the oven to 400°F.

Toss the peppers with the 2 tablespoons of the oil in a bowl and season with salt. Spread them out on a baking sheet and roast until cooked through and barely blistered, 10 to 12 minutes. Let cool. Chop ⅓ cup of roasted peppers. Reserve the rest of the peppers for the salad.

Combine the egg yolks, garlic, vinegar, mustard powder, and 1 teaspoon salt in a food processor and process until smooth. With the processor running, slowly add the remaining 1 cup of oil and process until emulsified, about 1 minute.

Add the crème fraîche, ketchup, Worcestershire, and Tabasco to the processor and process until well incorporated. Add the shallot and the ⅓ cup of chopped roasted peppers and process once more. Transfer the dressing to a bowl and stir in the dill pickles. Cover and store in the refrigerator for up to 3 days.

To make the salad: Bring a pot of water to a simmer over high heat and add enough salt so that the water tastes like the sea. Prepare an ice bath, also salty like the sea.

Drop the shrimp into the simmering water and cook until just pink, 30 to 40 seconds. Using a spider skimmer or similar tool, quickly transfer to the ice bath and let cool completely.

Arrange the lettuce on a serving platter or wide shallow bowl. Drizzle 1 cup of the dressing over the lettuce. In a small bowl, season the shrimp with a pinch of salt and a squirt of lemon juice and toss to coat. Place on top of the lettuce. Do the same with the crab. Top the lettuce with the halved eggs, the remaining whole roasted peppers, and dill. Serve with extra dressing on the side. Eat immediately.

PERFECT EGGS

BY WAY OF OUR FRIEND CHRIS FISCHER

"We need an egg-boiling recipe, don't we?"

So began our decision to include this landmark contribution to American culinaria. Chris Fischer, a friend of mine who is also an extremely handsome and thoughtful chef, won a James Beard Award for a book wherein he shared a recipe for boiled eggs. Said recipe was even featured by Martha Stewart. Prior to Chris's book, I assume Martha had given up on even attempting to boil eggs after so many years of disappointment and failure. His near-magical formula consists of putting eggs in boiling water for 7 minutes and then transferring them to an ice bath. Without his express permission, I've decided to adapt his recipe. My hope is that we will be featured on Goop, as I have been in love with Gwyneth Paltrow since I was thirteen. I am not sure if Chris felt similarly about Martha, and, understanding her egg dilemma, created the recipe as a way to her heart. He is very thoughtful.

The recipe key here is time. After a certain point of boiling, you are treading into smelly green crumbly yolk territory. There is a fine line between semi-soft-boiled and brutally punished.

    8 cups water
    Kosher salt
    4 eggs

Bring the water to a boil in a large saucepan.

Prepare an ice bath and add enough salt so that the water tastes like the sea.

Add the eggs to the boiling water.

Boil the eggs for not 7, but 8 minutes. (Adaptation, people.)

Immediately transfer the eggs to the ice bath and let cool completely.

Peel the eggs and half lengthwise.

Note: This recipe also works with hot dogs. If used for hot dogs, follow the cooking instructions and then transfer to buns instead of an ice bath. Do not peel your dogs.

AVOCADO AND CRISPY RICE

The dish is inspired by Vietnamese flavors, and the dressing is a version of *nuoc cham*, a sour-sweet-savory dipping sauce. As with most food items (hamburgers, toast, sushi, pancakes), you can turn it into California cuisine just by adding an avocado. Plan for one avocado per person if the fruit are small, and half an avocado if they are large.

If you don't have the time or desire to make all the components from scratch, this is a salad that lends itself well to shortcuts, as chile oil and puffed rice (unsweetened) are readily available in most markets.

A note on serving: At the restaurant, we put two avocado halves per plate, allowing two diners to share as an appetizer. For a group, you might want to do one big family-style platter. At home, it might be easier to put the avocado at the bottom of individual bowls and then layer the rest of the ingredients over them.

CRISPY RICE AND SHALLOTS

1 cup cooked brown rice

2 cups rice bran oil or other neutral oil, for frying

2 shallots, thinly sliced

1 tablespoon cornstarch

SALAD

¼ cup chile oil (page 221)

1 tablespoon pomegranate molasses

3 limes

1 tablespoon fish sauce

1 cup toasted unsweetened coconut flakes

Leaves from 1 bunch cilantro

4 ripe avocados

Kosher salt

½ cup pomegranate seeds

1 (2-inch) piece fresh ginger, peeled and minced

SERVES 4

To make the rice and shallots: Preheat the oven to 200°F. Line a baking sheet with parchment paper.

Spread the brown rice on the prepared baking sheet. Bake for 1 hour and then turn off the oven, and leave the rice in the oven for about 12 hours. The goal is to dry out the rice as best you can.

Heat the oil in a small saucepan over medium heat until it reaches 400°F. If the oil is not hot enough, the rice will not puff, instead leaving you with what will taste like burned glass. When the oil is hot, fry the rice in two batches, until puffed, about 15 seconds. Using a spider skimmer or other small strainer, remove the rice from the oil and drain on paper towels. Set aside.

Lightly dust the shallots with the cornstarch in a bowl and shake off any excess. Using the same oil and pot, reheat the oil over medium heat until it reaches 350°F. When the oil is hot, fry the shallots until they pop (be careful!), 20 to 30 seconds. Using a spider skimmer or other small strainer,

remove from the oil and drain on paper towels. Set aside.

To make the salad: Stir together the chile oil and pomegranate molasses in a small bowl or cup. Set aside.

Juice two of the limes into a small bowl. Cut the remaining lime in half and set aside.

In a large salad bowl, stir together the fish sauce and 2 tablespoons of the lime juice. Add the crispy rice and stir to evenly coat. Add the fried shallots, coconut flakes, and cilantro and toss together. Taste and adjust the seasoning with additional lime juice.

Slice the avocados in half. Remove the pits and, using a spoon, remove each avocado half from its skin. Put the avocados on your serving vessels of choice.

Sprinkle the avocados with salt and an additional squirt of lime juice. Spoon the rice mixture over the avocado. Dress with the chile oil mixture, and sprinkle with the pomegranate seeds and ginger. Add more lime juice, if desired. Eat immediately.

WINTER VEGETABLE SALAD

The challenge—and opportunity—of winter produce is to create something that's seasonal but still bright and fresh. This root vegetable salad hits both of those requirements, combining roasted and raw vegetables in a preserved lemon dressing.

The individual components in this salad can easily swap in and out for whatever is readily available. You want a combination of textures; cooked and raw, peeled and not.

1 lemon

1 cup neutral oil (such as safflower oil)

½ preserved lemon, seeded

2 tablespoons honey, or to taste

3 Chioggia beets, peeled

Kosher salt

3 carrots, peeled

3 parsnips, peeled

2 tablespoons extra-virgin olive oil

1 head Castelfranco or other hearty lettuce, leaves separated

1 fennel bulb, cored and sliced

1 celery rib, thinly sliced, plus ½ cup celery leaves (optional)

Leaves from 1 bunch flat-leaf parsley

1 cup salted roasted peanuts or other nuts, crushed

Veggie chips (optional)

SERVES 4

Zest and juice the lemon, and set aside. Blend the neutral oil, preserved lemon, honey, and three-fourths of the lemon juice in a blender. Taste and add more honey or lemon juice if necessary. The dressing should be a vibrant balance between saltiness, acidity, and sweetness.

Preheat the oven to 325°F.

Tightly wrap two of the beets in aluminum foil with the lemon zest and a pinch of salt. (I like to cook beets in the oven by wrapping them in aluminum foil with various other delicious things; it's pretty much the easiest cooking technique ever.) Cook the beets until fork tender but not soft, 45 to 60 minutes. Remove from the oven and let cool. When the beets are cool, cut into small chunks. Set aside.

Cut two of the carrots and two of the parsnips into uniform chunks.

Heat the olive oil in a sauté pan over medium-high heat. Add the parsnip and carrot chunks and cook, stirring occasionally, until they show color and are tender but not mushy, about 6 minutes. Remove from the pan and set aside in a large bowl and let cool.

Using a mandoline or a vegetable peeler, thinly shave the remaining beet, carrot, and parsnip. Add the raw vegetable shavings to the cooked vegetables. Add the lettuce, fennel, celery, celery leaves, and parsley and toss to combine.

Add half the dressing and toss until everything is evenly coated. Add the peanuts, season with salt, and toss again. Arrange on a platter or in a shallow bowl. Add more dressing, if desired. Garnish with veggie chips sprinkled over the salad. Eat immediately.

Note: When pan-roasting vegetables, make sure the vegetables are cut to roughly the same size and shape to ensure even cooking.

KALE SALADS ARE OVER

Kale salads are generally lame, but we felt like we had to include one because everyone else is doing it and people eat them and we are insecure serfs to our customers. Also, the salad we planned to photograph was accidentally served for a staff meal last night and we needed to take a photo today.

In all seriousness, the kale—or any hearty green—provides a nice medium to showcase the other components of this salad, especially late-spring produce. The amounts of cherries and asparagus here are forgiving; you can go as heavy or light as you like.

CILANTRO–PUMPKIN SEED DRESSING

1 cup pumpkin seeds

1 teaspoon coriander seeds

½ cup cider vinegar

2 cloves garlic

2 teaspoons kosher salt

1 cup picked cilantro leaves

2 cups neutral oil

TOASTED PUMPKIN SEEDS

1 teaspoon neutral oil (such as safflower oil)

½ cup pumpkin seeds

½ teaspoon kosher salt

SALAD

1 bunch kale, stemmed and torn into bite-size pieces

1 bunch (12 to 18 spears) asparagus, split lengthwise and cut into 2-inch segments

2 cups cherries, pitted and halved

¼ cup golden raisins

Juice of 1 lemon

½ teaspoon kosher salt

Handful of fresh cilantro leaves

SERVES 4

To make the dressing: In a small skillet over medium heat, toast the 1 cup pumpkin seeds and coriander seeds until fragrant, about 5 minutes. Pour the vinegar into a food processor or high-powered blender and add the garlic, 2 teaspoons salt, and cilantro. Puree and add the toasted seeds. Blend to combine. With the processor running, slowly pour in the 2 cups of oil and process until emulsified, about 1 minute.

To make the toasted pumpkin seeds: Heat the oil in a small skillet over medium-high heat. Add the ½ cup pumpkin seeds and ½ teaspoon salt and toast until fragrant, about 1 minute. Set aside and let cool.

To make the salad: Combine the kale and dressing in a large bowl and toss until evenly coated. Arrange the dressed kale on a serving platter or keep in the bowl.

In a second bowl, toss together the asparagus, cherries, raisins, lemon juice, and ½ teaspoon salt. Transfer to the platter and evenly distribute atop the kale. Scatter the toasted pumpkin seeds and cilantro over the top. Eat immediately.

SMOKY POTATO SALAD

When you really stop and think about it, potato salad is an American barbecue staple that, oddly, has nothing directly to do with the barbecue. More often than not, you buy it at a grocery store or deli, and if you do make it, there's no true connection to the great outdoors. So, why not use that fire you built for more than just grilling your meat shapes? Applying the coals to smoking things is a by-product benefit of grilling over live fire (see page 163). After boiling the potatoes, smoke them for a few minutes to add a hint of fire flavor to this mustardy, malty version of a German potato salad.

MUSTARD SEED DRESSING

½ cup yellow mustard seeds

3 tablespoons fennel seeds

1 cup malt vinegar

1 teaspoon kosher salt

1 teaspoon sugar

3 tablespoons peanut oil

SALAD

Kosher salt

1 cup fresh English peas (from about 1 pound unshelled)

20 fingerling potatoes (about 2 pounds), unpeeled

2 cups snap peas, trimmed and cut into bite-size pieces

2 summer squashes, cut into ⅛-inch slices

Juice of ½ lemon

SERVES 2 TO 4

To make the dressing: Combine the mustard seeds and fennel seeds in a small bowl or jar that can hold a little more than 1 cup of liquid. Put the vinegar in a small pot and bring to a simmer over high heat. Add the salt and sugar, remove from the heat, and stir until dissolved. Pour the vinegar mixture over the seeds and let soak for at least 1 hour, and up to 12 hours. Add the peanut oil and stir to combine. Store in the refrigerator indefinitely.

To make the salad: Bring a large pot of water to a boil over high heat and add enough salt so that the water tastes like the sea. Prepare an ice bath, also salty like the sea.

Drop the English peas into the boiling water and cook until warmed through, 10 to 15 seconds. Using a small strainer, quickly transfer the peas to the ice bath and let cool completely. Drain in a colander and et dry on paper towels.

Bring the same pot of water back up to a boil. Add the potatoes and boil until they are tender and can be pierced with a fork, 20 to 25 minutes. Drain in a colander and let cool.

Transfer a smoking ember to a sealed container, like a large pot, or prepare your stove-top smoker. Working in batches, add the potatoes to the smoker, cover, and smoke for 3 to 4 minutes, until they taste smoky.

When cool enough to handle, cut the potatoes into bite-size chunks. Combine the potatoes, snap peas, squash, and English peas in a large bowl, add two-thirds of the dressing, and toss until everything is evenly coated. Taste and season with lemon juice, as needed. Add more dressing, if desired. Transfer to a bowl or platter. Eat immediately or refrigerate, covered, as it will keep for a few hours if you're traveling to a picnic.

BEAN SALAD

In the restaurant, we make this salad with nine different kinds of beans, each prepared separately because they have different cooking times. Everyone has to shuck beans. At some point, we may ask customers to shuck while they wait for their food. Such a veritable menagerie of shell and snap beans is not quite realistic for a home cook, or the restaurant actually, so this recipe simply calls for two types. Use as many as you have the patience to seek out and shuck. Canned or dried beans will work, too, though your cooking times will change; fresh beans are markedly better.

VINAIGRETTE

½ cup extra-virgin olive oil

¼ cup sherry vinegar

1 gypsy pepper or other red sweet pepper, seeded and finely diced

1 shallot, minced

2 tablespoons freshly squeezed lemon juice

1 teaspoon kosher salt

Freshly ground black pepper

SALAD

1½ to 2 cups fresh shell beans (such as cannellini, borlotti, or flageolet; from about 1 pound unshelled)

Salt

8 ounces snap beans (such as wax beans, Romano beans, or haricots verts)

2 cups assorted cherry tomatoes, halved

1 tablespoon fresh oregano leaves

¼ cup flat-leaf parsley leaves

1 cup aioli (page 219)

SERVES 4

To make the vinaigrette: Combine the oil, vinegar, gypsy pepper, shallot, lemon juice, and salt in a small bowl and stir well. Season with black pepper. Set aside, stirring again before use.

To make the salad: Put the shell beans in a pot, add enough water to cover, and bring to a boil over high heat. Lower the heat to a simmer and cook until tender. Cooking times will vary by bean type, but most should take 20 to 30 minutes. Remove from the heat, add a pinch of salt, and let the beans cool in their cooking liquid. When ready to use, drain the shell beans.

Bring a second pot of water to a boil over high heat and add enough salt so that the water tastes like the sea. Prepare an ice bath, also salty like the sea.

Drop the snap beans into the boiling water and cook until barely tender, about 1 minute. Using a small strainer, transfer the beans to the ice bath and let cool completely. Drain in a colander and let dry on paper towels.

In a large bowl, combine the shell beans and vinaigrette, toss until evenly coated, and let sit for 15 minutes. Using a slotted spoon, transfer the shell beans to a platter or serving bowl, reserving the vinaigrette. Add the snap beans and tomatoes to the vinaigrette and toss until evenly coated. Season with salt. Add the snap beans and tomatoes to the shell beans and toss gently to combine. Sprinkle the oregano and parsley over the top. Serve with the aioli on the side, and encourage diners to use it as a condiment.

CAULIFLOWER AND FAVA SALAD

Cooking a whole head of cauliflower like a piece of meat—whether in the oven or straight on the grill—is an easy and delicious technique, and this dish might possibly the simplest salad recipe in the book. In the late spring and early summer months, favas are at their best—all they need is a quick dip in boiling water to cook. Mix with salty feta, bright lemon juice, and a bunch of veggies, and you've got a hearty side salad that easily transports and holds up for hours. (This recipe uses fresh garbanzo beans, but the canned version will work, too.)

1 head cauliflower (any color), trimmed
2 tablespoons extra-virgin olive oil
Kosher salt
1 pound shelled fava beans
(2 to 3 pounds in the pod)
½ pound fresh garbanzo beans
2 lemons
2 teaspoons nigella seeds
6 ounces feta cheese, crumbled
Freshly ground black pepper

SERVES 4

Dress the whole head of cauliflower with 1 tablespoon of the olive oil and 1 teaspoon salt.

To cook on a grill: Place the cauliflower over medium-high heat and cook until nice and charred on the outside but tender inside, 45 to 60 minutes. The inner part of the cauliflower should be tender enough to easily pierce with a fork.

To roast in an oven: Preheat the oven to 375°F. Put the cauliflower in a baking dish and cook until the inner part is tender enough to easily pierce with a fork, about 60 minutes.

Let the cauliflower cool, and then trim and cut into bite-size florets. Set aside.

Bring a pot of water to a boil over high heat and add enough salt so that the water tastes like the sea. Prepare an ice bath, also salty like the sea.

Drop the fava beans into the boiling water and cook until barely tender, about 15 seconds. Using a small strainer, transfer to the ice bath and let cool. Drain in a colander, peel, and set aside.

Using the same water and ice bath, repeat with the garbanzos, if fresh. They will need to cook about 30 seconds in the boiling water. (If using canned garbanzos, do not cook, just drain and rinse.)

In a large bowl, combine the cauliflower and garbanzos. Finely grate the zest of the lemons into the bowl, and then juice the lemons and add the juice to the bowl. Add the remaining 1 tablespoon olive oil and 1 teaspoon salt, toss until everything is evenly coated, and let sit for 10 to 15 minutes.

While the vegetables sit, in a small pan over medium-high heat, toast the nigella seeds for 30 seconds, until fragrant. Set aside.

Add favas and feta to the vegetables, and gently toss to combine. Taste and season with more salt, as needed. Arrange the salad on a large platter or individual bowls. Sprinkle the nigella seeds and pepper over the top. Eat immediately.

CHAPTER 6

DRINKS

DRINKS

DRINKS

DRINKS

DRINKS

DRINKS

DRINKS

DRINKS

KB CARBONATED MARGARITA

This is the only cocktail that is always on the restaurant's menu, dating all the way back to the early days. The carbonated margarita has somehow become a signature, and we sell twice as much of it as any other cocktail. Perhaps it's because it is a light and refreshing twist on the margarita, the perfect pairing for juicy burgers and salty fries. Or maybe it's because we originally called it "Carbonated Motherfucking Margarita," a most lyrical phrase if there was ever one, and one that may have helped land some of our earliest major national press (thanks, *GQ*). At the restaurant, we use a carbonation system to add bubbles to the drinks, but at home, using sparkling water works, too.

10 ounces tequila or mezcal
6 ounces sparkling water
4 ounces freshly squeezed lime juice
2 ounces light agave syrup
1 pinch of kosher salt
Ice cubes, for serving
4 orange twists

MAKES 4 COCKTAILS, SERVED ON THE ROCKS

Combine the tequila, sparkling water, lime juice, agave syrup, and salt in a pitcher. Stir well to combine. Serve over ice in a rocks glass, Collins glass, compostable cup, or whatever you prefer, with an orange twist.

Note: If using a soda siphon, replace sparkling water with water and build the cocktail in the soda siphon.

DANDY

A take on the Manhattan cocktail, the Dandy adds an additional touch of complexity to the usual variation. The whiskey side of the equation stays the same, but the complementary side gets an addition of Amaro Lucano and aquavit to the usual sweet vermouth. Amaro Lucano in particular is a medium-style liqueur that gives the cocktail a little more body and some spice to accentuate the vermouth's sweetness.

1½ ounces rye whiskey
½ ounce aquavit
½ ounce sweet vermouth
¼ ounce Amaro Lucano
2 dashes Angostura bitters
Ice cubes, for chilling
1 thick piece of lemon peel
Orange twist, for garnish

MAKES 1 COCKTAIL, SERVED UP

Combine the rye, aquavit, vermouth, Amaro Lucano, and bitters in a mixing glass filled with ice. Stir until chilled and then strain into a chilled coupe. Rub the lemon peel around the rim of the glass, twist it over the drink to release the oils, and discard. Garnish with the orange twist.

KB MARTINI

Usually, martinis go heavy on the gin (or vodka). The KB Martini takes a more temperate route, upping the dry vermouth ratio significantly, making for an easier drinking experience. The kombu infusion is an optional step that brings an extra hint of salinity and umami to the finished drink. One might even say that the kombu gives the martini an extra . . . twist.

2 ounces gin
¾ ounce kombu vermouth (see Note) or Dolin dry vermouth
3 dashes citrus bitters
Ice cubes, for chilling
Cocktail onion or a pickled ramp, if you're ambitious, for garnish
Lemon twist, for garnish

MAKES 1 COCKTAIL, SERVED UP

Combine the gin, vermouth, and bitters in a mixing glass filled with ice. Stir until chilled and then strain into a chilled coupe or martini glass. Garnish with the cocktail onion and lemon twist.

Note: To make kombu vermouth, gently clean ½ ounce of kombu with a damp cloth. Cut slits into the kombu and put it in a container. Add 1 (750 ml) bottle of vermouth and let steep in the refrigerator for 8 hours. Discard the kombu, straining the vermouth back in the bottle, if needed. Store in the refrigerator indefinitely, and drink with all future martinis.

SUNSHINE SOUR

Sours are a traditional cocktail family, a genre of drinks characterized by a central liquor, a citrus component, and a sweetener. The margarita and paloma are its best-known examples. Here, gin may be the base but it's a citrus-forward drink, featuring both lemon and orange juices. The ingredient that balances it all out, with just the slightest bitterness, is the Cappelletti, an Italian aperitivo liqueur. It's a bright, syrupy red like Campari, but has a lighter, sweeter, and less overpowering flavor. And it is lower ABV, making for a daytime, easy drinker.

1 ounce gin
1 ounce Cappelletti
1 ounce freshly squeezed lemon juice
½ ounce freshly squeezed orange juice
½ ounce gum syrup (such as Small Hands Foods brand)
Ice cubes, for chilling and serving
Orange twist or edible flower, for garnish

MAKES 1 COCKTAIL, SERVED ON THE ROCKS

Combine the gin, Cappelletti, lemon juice, orange juice, and gum syrup in a cocktail shaker filled with ice. Shake until chilled and then strain into a highball or double-rocks glass over ice. Garnish with the orange twist or, if you're feeling happy, an edible flower.

FALLING AND LAUGHING

During the autumnal season, take a stand
and do the right thing. Instead of drinking
a pumpkin spice latte and supporting
the dark, corporate, genetically modified
pumpkin-shaped shadow sweeping across
the world, embrace the essence of fall by
making and drinking this cocktail. Maple!
Ginger! Apples! It's like a forest of cascading
red and orange leaves, but in a glass.

1½ ounces bourbon
¾ ounce freshly squeezed lemon juice
½ ounce ginger juice
½ ounce maple syrup
¼ ounce Amaro Lucano
Ice cubes, for chilling and serving
2½ ounces Brittany cider, like Domaine
Johanna Cecillon Cidre Divona
Orange twist, for garnish

MAKES 1 COCKTAIL, SERVED ON THE ROCKS

Combine the bourbon, lemon juice, ginger juice,
maple syrup, and Amaro Lucano in a cocktail
shaker filled with ice. Shake until chilled and then
strain into a Collins glass over ice. Top off with the
cider. Garnish with the orange twist.

WANDERLUST

Vermouth cocktails are a lower-alcohol
option for those seeking a spirit-forward
drink. Here, we use Cocchi Americano
Rosa, a quinine-flavored, slightly bittersweet aperitif wine from Italy that can also
be used in martinis and Manhattans.

3 ounces sparkling water
2 ounces vermouth (such as Cocchi
Americano Rosa)
½ ounce mezcal (such as Del Maguey Vida)
1 teaspoon freshly squeezed lemon juice
Ice cubes, for serving
Orange twist, for garnish
Lemon wheel, for garnish

MAKES 1 COCKTAIL, SERVED ON THE ROCKS

Combine the sparkling water, vermouth, mezcal,
and lemon juice in a highball glass. Fill with ice.
Gently stir until chilled. Garnish with the orange
twist and lemon wheel.

BLACK SUN

Coffee, a whole egg, orange, booze. It's all the breakfast you'll ever need, a one-stop shop for caffeine, protein, and alcohol. Have a very good/bad morning.

2½ ounces iced coffee
(preferably cold-brewed)
1½ ounces Jamaican black rum
(such as Hamilton)
¾ ounce Amaro CioCiaro
½ ounce simple syrup (see below)
1 egg
Ice cubes, for chilling and serving
Orange twist, for garnish

MAKES 1 COCKTAIL, SERVED ON THE ROCKS

Combine the iced coffee, rum, Amaro CioCiaro, simple syrup, and egg in a cocktail shaker and shake well—without ice, this technique is known as a "dry shake." Add ice and shake again until chilled. Strain into a Collins glass. Add ice. Garnish with the orange peel.

How to Make Simple Syrup

To make simple syrup, combine equal parts sugar and hot water and mix until sugar dissolves. Cool before using and store up to 1 month in the fridge.

To make a sweeter simple syrup, combine two parts sugar to one part water and proceed as above.

CLOUD 29

Though there are clear nods to the Negroni—the gin, the Campari, the vermouth—the Cloud 29 ratios are tweaked, moving it away from the Negroni's signature equal-thirds structure. This cocktail leans more on gin, and sneaks in a few gentian accents and herbal flavors in the form of absinthe, Leopold Bros. Aperitivo (an American-made cousin of Campari), and Bonal (a French quinine wine).

1¼ ounces gin
¾ ounce Campari
½ ounce Bonal
½ ounce Cocchi Vermouth di Torino
¼ ounce Leopold Bros. Aperitivo
1 dash absinthe
1 piece lemon peel
Ice cubes, for chilling and serving
Orange twist, for garnish

MAKES 1 COCKTAIL, SERVED ON THE ROCKS

Combine the gin, Campari, Bonal, vermouth, Aperitivo, absinthe, and lemon peel in a mixing glass filled with ice. Stir until chilled and then strain into an old-fashioned glass or rocks glass over ice. Garnish with the orange peel.

Drinks

Old Beef, Young Wine

By Bradford Taylor, owner of Ordinaire wine bar in Oakland, California

I eat Kronnerburgers, but only when I'm drunk. For the most part, I avoid them on principle. I got to know Chris when he was cooking bistro pop-ups at Ordinaire, my wine bar and shop in Oakland. And seeing the kind of food he was able to put out of that cramped space, the last thing I wanted him to serve me out of his fancy kitchen on Piedmont Avenue was a burger. Seemed like a waste to me. I'd rather eat his leeks vinaigrette with poached oysters, chervil, and egg. Or soft shell crab with cucumber vichyssoise. Squab terrine with savory and apricot mustard. Tête de veau with sauce ravigote and haricots verts.

So when Chris told me that he had finally signed a lease and was opening Kronnerburger, I was a little happy for him, but I was mostly pissed. Pissed that he was going to cook hamburgers. Hamburgers? Seriously?

But, of course, I was missing the point. While I wanted Chris to flaunt his technique, he decided instead to package all that imaginative complexity in simpler forms. I'm not sure people really understand how much physical and intellectual labor goes into producing his burger and fries—which is, frustratingly, the whole point.

Natural wine offers a theoretical parallel in the way that it actively obscures the difficulty and precariousness of its creation by celebrating a culture of thoughtless bacchanalian consumption. The ideology of the natural-wine "movement" centers on the belief that wine has the power to reproduce and affirm the human desire for pleasure, unmoored from the rationalization that has come to dominate wine culture. By contrast, conventional wine tends to obsess over the science of glassware, procedures of analytical appreciation, and objective systems of judgments. Wordsworth might have said, "we murder to dissect," and then slammed a glass of Gamay in five iambic gulps.

So what wine goes with a hamburger? Most people would instinctively reach for something dark, tannic. A Cab! A Malbec! I've never really been into wines that stand up to food, as if they are locked in some kind of Napoleonic battle sequence.

Kronnerburgers are full of fat, salt, and funk; less akin to something you would find at a diner, and more like something you might find in a Lyonnais bouchon. So the wine list is what I imagine a French diner would serve—lots of Beaujolais, whites from Macon, some denser wines from the Northern Rhône and the Roussillon,

and a selection of Loire bubbles. The wines are fresh and zesty, full of acidity and crunchy fruit, simple in the best way.

But to be honest, natural wine is nothing if it gets distracted by the discourse of "pairing" and forgets that, at its core, it's about making people feel more in touch with each other and the earth—more alive. And this is what Chris's food has always been about to me. Eat, drink, and be more alive.

LEMONADE

A little salt adds balance to the tart and sweet. Enjoy on your porch, real or imagined, in a rocking chair.

4 ounces water
2 ounces freshly squeezed lemon juice
1½ ounces sweet simple syrup
(2:1 sugar to water ratio, see page 193
1 pinch of kosher salt
Ice cubes, for chilling and serving
Lemon wheel, for garnish

MAKES 1 DRINK

Combine the water, lemon juice, simple syrup, and salt in a cocktail shaker filled with ice. Shake until chilled and then strain into a highball glass. Add ice. Garnish with the lemon wheel.

CUCUMBER CILANTRO COOLER

If a soda jerk served spa water, it would be the Cucumber Cilantro Cooler.

1½ ounces cucumber juice
1½ ounces freshly squeezed lime juice
1½ ounces simple syrup (see page 193)
Handful of fresh cilantro leaves
1 pinch of kosher salt
Ice cubes, for chilling and serving
4 ounces sparkling water
Lime wheel, for garnish

MAKES 1 DRINK

Combine the cucumber juice, lime juice, simple syrup, cilantro, and salt in a cocktail shaker filled with ice. Shake until chilled and then strain into a highball glass over ice. Top off with the sparkling water. Garnish with the lime wheel.

ORANGE CREAM SODA

The Creamsicle of your childhood, in drink form. Be very careful, as this may be the most addictive recipe in this chapter.

4 ounces sparkling water
1 ounce Orange-Vanilla Syrup (recipe follows)
½ ounce heavy cream
¼ ounce freshly squeezed lemon juice
Ice cubes, for chilling and serving
Orange twist, for garnish

MAKES 1 DRINK

Combine the sparkling water, orange-vanilla syrup, cream, and lemon juice in a cocktail shaker filled with ice. Shake until chilled and the strain into a highball glass. Add ice. Garnish with the lemon wheel.

ORANGE-VANILLA SYRUP

1 cup sugar
1 cup freshly squeezed strained orange juice
Peel of ½ orange
¼ teaspoon vanilla extract

MAKES 1 CUP

Combine the sugar, orange juice, and orange peel in a saucepan and cook over medium heat until the sugar is dissolved and a syrup forms,

8 to 10 minutes. (The temperature, if you're using a candy thermometer, should reach 165°F.) Remove from the heat and let cool. When cool, stir in the vanilla. Use immediately or store in the refrigerator indefinitely.

GINGER TURMERIC SODA

Freshness and brightness are sought-after qualities behind our bar, especially for the booze-free drinks. If you don't have a juicer to make your own ginger and turmeric juices, both are often available at health food stores and specialty grocers.

1½ ounces sweet simple syrup
(2:1 sugar to water ratio, see page 193)
1½ ounces fresh lime juice
½ ounce ginger juice
¼ ounce turmeric juice
Ice cubes, for chilling and serving
4 ounces sparkling water
Lime and/or lemon wheel, for garnish

MAKES 1 DRINK

Combine the simple syrup, lime juice, ginger juice, and turmeric juice in a cocktail shaker filled with ice. Shake until chilled and then strain into a highball glass over ice. Top off with the sparkling water. Garnish with the citrus wheel(s).

STRAWBERRY MINT LIME SODA

Imagine it, a strawberry soda that tastes like real strawberries, not some cough-syrup simulacrum. The strawberry syrup can be added to margaritas—carbonated or not—or enjoyed swirled into a milkshake. Or just pair it with lime juice and bubbles as in this tart-sweet concoction.

1½ ounces strawberry syrup (see Note)
1½ ounces freshly squeezed lime juice
Handful of fresh mint leaves, plus a few
for garnish
Ice cubes, for chilling and serving
4 ounces sparkling water
Lime wheel, for garnish

MAKES 1 DRINK

Combine the strawberry syrup, lime juice, and mint in a cocktail shaker filled with ice. Shake until chilled and then strain into a highball glass over ice. Top off with the sparkling water. Garnish with mint leaves and the lime wheel.

Note: To make strawberry syrup, clean and hull strawberries. Any amount is okay! Puree in a blender and then strain through a fine-mesh strainer into a measuring cup. Note the volume. Pour the juice into a pot and add an equal amount of sugar. Bring to a boil over medium-high heat and then turn to low heat, until thickened. Stir until fully incorporated. Cool before using. Can be stored in the refrigerator for up to 1 week.

CHAPTER 7

DESSERTS

HONEY PIE

Burgers and pies have always been inextricably linked in the American diner. From the neon drive-ins of Southern California to the small-town luncheonettes of northern Idaho to the 24-hour coffee shops of Queens, each one is home to a case of pies, ready and waiting (by the slice, of course) behind the counter. Cherry. Apple. French silk. Lemon meringue. The pie case, just far enough out of sight to require a squint to see the flavors, was a beacon for those finishing up their burger and shake. Without a doubt, honey pie has been the flagship dessert at the restaurant, and for good reason. It is a really, really good pie—rich, decadent, sweet, and salty.

1 pie shell (recipe follows)

⅔ cup (150 grams) unsalted butter, melted

⅔ cup (133 grams) vanilla sugar (see Note)

1 tablespoon plus ¾ teaspoon (10 grams) all-purpose flour

1 teaspoon (5 grams) kosher salt

1 cup (332 grams) honey

4 large eggs (200 grams)

⅔ cup (160 grams) heavy cream

1 tablespoon plus 1 teaspoon (20 grams) cider vinegar

Whipped cream, for serving

MAKES ONE 9-INCH PIE

Preheat the oven to 400°F.

Take the pie shell straight from the freezer and bake for 25 minutes. Remove from the oven and let cool.

While the pie shell is baking, whisk together the butter, vanilla, sugar, flour, and salt in a large bowl. Add the honey and whisk gently to combine. In another bowl, whisk together the eggs and cream with a fork. Gradually combine the egg mixture and the flour mixture, being careful not to over-mix, which will incorporate too many air bubbles. Whisk in the vinegar. (If not using immediately, transfer the custard to an airtight container and refrigerate for up to 2 days. If refrigerating, gently stir to combine once again before using.)

When the pie shell is baked and cooled, pass the custard through a fine-mesh sieve over the pie shell, pressing with a spoon or ladle to extract as much of the custard as possible. Bake the pie until the custard is puffed and brown, about 35 minutes. Let cool to room temperature.

The pie doesn't need to be refrigerated, but you can. It will keep covered with plastic wrap for 1 week. Serve cold or at room temperature, cut by the slice, with a dollop of whipped cream.

Note: To make vanilla sugar, measure 2 cups (400 grams) sugar into a sealable container. Split one vanilla bean lengthwise down the middle, scraping its seeds into the sugar. Bury the bean pod in the sugar and let sit for at least a few days or up to several weeks. Substitute vanilla sugar anywhere you would use normal sugar. If you don't have the luxury of planning ahead for this recipe, make instant vanilla sugar by mixing ½ teaspoon (3 grams) vanilla extract into ⅔ cup (133 grams) sugar.

CONTINUED

PIE SHELL

1 cup (125 grams) all-purpose flour

¼ teaspoon (2 grams) kosher salt

½ cup (113 grams) cold unsalted butter, cut into ¹⁄₁₆-inch slices

¼ cup (60 grams) cold water

MAKES ONE 9-INCH PIE SHELL

Stir together the flour and salt in a bowl and then sift it onto a flat work surface. Press the butter slices into the flour with the heel of your hand. Transfer the flour-butter mixture to a large bowl, add the water, and gently mix with a wooden spoon. Transfer to the work surface and press the dough into a rectangle, cover in plastic wrap, and refrigerate for 30 minutes.

Using a rolling pin in only one direction (that is, repeatedly roll only one way; don't go back and forth), roll out the rectangle of dough on a very lightly floured work surface until it is ⅛ inch thick and doubled in length, adding as little flour as possible to prevent sticking. Fold the extended part of the rectangle back onto the dough, re-forming the original rectangle. Rotate the dough 90 degrees and repeat this process another three times, so that each side gets rolled out. Cover in the plastic wrap once again and refrigerate for another 30 minutes.

When the dough is completely chilled, roll it into a 12-inch round and mold into a 9-inch pie pan. Using your hands, press the dough firmly into the pie pan, ensuring an even distribution so the whole pan is covered. Trim and crimp the edges, if desired. Cover with plastic wrap and store in the freezer indefinitely.

DEVIL'S FOOD CAKE

I have no idea what designates a "devil's food" cake, but the name sounds way better than "layered chocolate cake." It's a twentieth-century classic, usually a towering cake with either a white or chocolate frosting. Here, the typical dense chocolate cake is buffered by a caramel ganache and brown sugar meringue. For our version, a six-layer number, you'll need three 9-inch cake pans; you can make the meringue while the cake bakes, but the ganache should be made ahead of time.

CARAMEL GANACHE

2 cups (452 grams) unsalted butter

4 cups (800 grams) granulated sugar

4 cups (960 grams) heavy cream

2 teaspoons (10 grams) vanilla extract

2 teaspoons (10 grams) kosher salt

18 ounces (510 grams) bittersweet (68% cacao) chocolate

BROWN SUGAR MERINGUE

⅓ cup (85 grams) egg whites

¾ cup (160 grams) packed brown sugar

¼ teaspoon (2 grams) salt

1 teaspoon (5 grams) vanilla extract

CAKES

2⅓ cups plus 2 tablespoons (300 grams) all-purpose flour

1 cup plus 1 tablespoon (96 grams) natural cocoa powder

2 teaspoons (10 grams) baking soda

¾ teaspoon (3 grams) baking powder

½ teaspoon (3 grams) kosher salt

1¾ cups plus 2 tablespoons (378 grams) granulated sugar

⅔ cup (168 grams) lightly beaten eggs

2 teaspoons (8 grams) vanilla extract

1 cup plus 1 tablespoon (256 grams) mayonnaise

1⅓ cups (315 grams) water

MAKES ONE 9-INCH CAKE

To make the ganache: In a small saucepan over medium-high heat, melt the butter. When the butter has melted, add the granulated sugar and turn the heat to medium-low. Whisking gently, cook until the mixture reaches a dark amber color and is barely smoking, about 5 minutes. Add about one-third of the cream and whisk until smooth. Add the rest of the cream in another two additions, continuing to whisk to create a smooth mixture. Add the vanilla and salt, mix to incorporate, and remove from the heat.

Pass the mixture through a fine-mesh strainer into a bowl. Add the chocolate and let sit for up to 3 hours before using. If you won't use it sooner than 3 hours, cover and refrigerate; bring back to room temperature before filling cake.

To make the meringue: Using a water bath or double boiler (that is, a small pot or heatproof bowl inside a pot of water on the stove), heat all ingredients, while stirring, until warm to the touch and the sugar is dissolved. Using an electric mixer or similar instrument, whip, starting on low speed and gradually increasing the mixer speed, until stiff peaks form. Set aside.

CONTINUED

DEVIL'S FOOD CAKE, CONTINUED

To make the cakes: Preheat the oven to 350°F. Butter three 9-inch cake pans and line the bottoms with parchment paper.

In a large bowl, sift the flour, cocoa powder, baking soda, baking powder, and salt. Mix to combine.

In a stand mixer using the paddle attachment, combine the granulated sugar, eggs, and vanilla on low speed until combined. Increase the speed to medium and mix for 5 minutes, then increase to high speed and mix for another 5 minutes. Add the mayonnaise and mix on medium speed, until combined.

Add one-fourth of the flour mixture to the mixer bowl and mix, and then add one-fourth of the water and mix. Continue to add the flour mixture and water, alternating between the two, while mixing, until both are fully incorporated. Divide the batter among the prepared cake pans. Bake until a cake tester or toothpick inserted into the center of a cake comes out clean, about 30 minutes. Let cool.

Cut each of the three cakes in half horizontally. Place one layer on a serving platter and spread about 1 cup of the ganache on it. Add a second cake layer and, working one layer at a time, repeat the process until all six layers are stacked. Use the remaining ganache to frost the top and sides of the cake. Put the meringue in a pastry bag (or plastic bag with the corner cut out) and frost the top edge of the cake. If you really want to be fancy, burn the meringue with a kitchen torch. Serve immediately or store covered in the refrigerator for up to 1 week.

DOUGHNUT MUFFINS

Do you like doughnuts, but don't feel like frying your breakfast? These doughnut muffins are the answer. Top with all your favorite doughnut fillings and toppings: maple glaze, strawberry jam, chocolate, sprinkles, Horsey Sauce, and so on. Doughnuts are not just for breakfast.

1½ cups (340 grams) unsalted butter, at room temperature, plus ¼ cup (57 grams), for dipping

1¾ cups (350 grams) sugar, plus 1 cup (200 grams), for finishing

4 large eggs (200 grams), at room temperature

3 cups (385 grams) all-purpose flour

2¾ cups (385 grams) cake flour

1 tablespoon plus 2 teaspoons (25 grams) baking powder

½ teaspoon (3 grams) baking soda

1¾ teaspoons (10 grams) kosher salt, plus 1 pinch for finishing

1 teaspoon (2 grams) grated nutmeg

1⅔ cups (400 grams) milk, at room temperature

½ cup (120 grams) buttermilk, at room temperature

1 tablespoon (8 grams) ground cinnamon, for finishing

MAKES ABOUT 12 MUFFINS

Preheat the oven to 350°F.

In a stand mixer fitted with the paddle attachment, combine the 1½ cups butter and 1¾ cups sugar on low speed until blended. Beat in the eggs, one at a time, until just combined.

In a large bowl, sift together the all-purpose flour, cake flour, baking powder, baking soda, salt, and nutmeg. In a second, smaller bowl, combine the milk and buttermilk. Add one-fourth of the flour mixture to the butter mixture and stir by hand. Add one-third of the milk mixture and stir until combined. Repeat with the remaining flour and milk mixtures, alternating to ensure an even mix, and stir together until smooth. (If not using immediately, cover and store in the refrigerator for up to 3 days.)

When ready to bake, generously grease a muffin tin. Using an ice cream scoop or large spoon, fill each muffin cup to the edge with batter. Bake until firm to the touch and light golden, about 30 minutes, rotating the tin halfway through. Set aside.

While the muffins cool, combine the cinnamon with the remaining 1 cup sugar and pinch of salt to make a cinnamon-sugar mixture. Melt the remaining ¼ cup butter in a small saucepan.

When the muffins are just cool enough to handle, remove them from the tin, dip them in the melted butter, and then roll in cinnamon sugar. Eat immediately or store covered at room temperature for up to 2 days.

PASSION FRUIT BARS

Why settle for boring old lemon bars when there is a planet's worth of fruits to turn into bars? (Sorry, lemon bars.) Any fruit puree can be swapped in for the passion fruit here—try mango or strawberry.

3½ cups (450 grams) all-purpose flour

1 cup (125 grams) confectioners' sugar

⅓ cup (50 grams) cornstarch

1¾ teaspoons (10 grams) kosher salt, plus 1 pinch for the filling

1¼ cups (280 grams) cold unsalted butter, cut into small pieces

2⅓ cups (466 grams) granulated sugar

7 large eggs (350 grams)

1½ cups (330 grams) passion fruit puree or other fruit puree

½ cup (120 grams) water

MAKES ABOUT 24 BARS

Preheat the oven to 375°F. Line a rimmed 13 by 18-inch baking sheet with parchment paper.

Combine 3¼ cups (400 grams) of the flour, the confectioners' sugar, cornstarch, salt, and butter in a food processor and process until a crumbly dough forms. Press the dough evenly into the bottom of the prepared pan. Bake until golden brown, about 30 minutes. Remove from the oven and let the crust cool completely. Lower the oven temperature to 350°F.

In a large bowl, stir together the granulated sugar and remaining ¼ cup (44 grams) flour. Add the eggs, puree, water, and pinch of salt. Strain through a fine-mesh sieve into a bowl.

Pour the filling into the cooled crust and bake until set, about 15 minutes. Remove from the oven and let cool completely before cutting into bars. Store refrigerated for up to 2 days.

FRUIT SALAD

Like a chopped salad, fruit salad is more of a mix-and-match situation. A kaleidoscope of textures and flavors—soft, fleshy, sweet, tart—all brought together by a binding coconut cream sauce. Because sometimes after eating burgers and bone marrow and fried potatoes, fresh fruit sounds like a responsible decision.

1 cup coconut cream (either from a can of coconut cream or scooped from the solids of a can of coconut milk), whipped

½ teaspoon sugar

2 oranges

1 peach, pitted and cut into bite-size pieces

2 cups fresh blackberries

2 cups fresh blueberries

2 cups fresh strawberries, hulled and halved

Leaves from 1 bunch basil or shiso

SERVES 2 TO 4

In a metal bowl, combine the coconut cream and sugar. Using an electric mixer or a whisk, whip the mixture until your desired level of fluffiness is achieved.

Cut the oranges into supremes or wedges. To supreme the citrus, cut off the rind and pith, essentially revealing the fruit inside. Following the membrane of each individual segment as closely as possible, make two slices in each segment; the wedge of fruit should pop out, leaving the membrane attached. Reserve the fruit.

In a large bowl, combine all the fruits and mix. Add the whipped coconut cream and gently mix. Transfer to a serving bowl or platter. Garnish with basil. Eat immediately.

BACON-FAT BLONDIES

It's like brownies and chocolate chip cookies had a baby and covered it in bacon. These blondies are chewy, sweet but not too sweet, rich, and gooey—and they're a perennial crowd-pleaser. The bacon fat contributes smoky flavor and extra delicious texture. Additional butter can be substituted for the pork averse.

¾ cup (150 grams) granulated sugar

3¾ cups (480 grams) all-purpose flour

2¾ teaspoons (12 grams) baking powder

2 teaspoons (12 grams) kosher salt

1 cup plus 1 tablespoon (250 grams) unsalted butter

1¼ cups (250 grams) rendered bacon fat

4 large eggs (200 grams)

2¾ cups (600 grams) packed brown sugar

1 tablespoon (13 grams) vanilla extract

9 ounces (255 grams) milk chocolate (53% cacao) disks or chips

MAKES ABOUT 24 BLONDIES

Line a large rimmed baking sheet or baking pan with parchment paper or a silicone mat.

In a saucepan, cook the granulated sugar over medium heat, stirring frequently and making sure to avoid scorching. The mixture should turn into a liquid in 7 to 8 minutes. When it starts to take on an amber color, another minute or two, immediately remove it from the heat and pour the caramel onto the baking sheet, spreading it as thinly as you can before it sets. Let cool, then break into bite-size shards. Set aside.

Preheat the oven to 350°F. Line a 13 by 18-inch baking pan with parchment paper or coat with vegetable oil spray.

Sift the flour, baking powder, and salt into a bowl. Set aside.

In a saucepan, melt the butter and bacon fat over medium heat. Remove from the heat, let cool slightly, and set aside.

In a large bowl, whisk together the eggs, brown sugar, and vanilla. Add the butter-bacon mixture and whisk until combined. Using a wooden spoon or spatula, gently fold in the flour mixture. Last but not least, fold in the chocolate. Spread the batter evenly in the pan and top with the caramel shards.

Bake until the blondies are golden brown and a toothpick inserted into the center comes out clean, about 30 minutes. Remove from the oven and let cool completely before cutting into bars. Store covered at room temperature for up to 3 days.

VEGAN COCONUT SORBET

No cows were harmed in the making of this refreshing frozen dessert. Think of this basic coconut sorbet as a blank canvas of sorts. It's good on its own, but it can also serve as a base to add any variety of flavor infusions, such as mint, basil, tarragon, or vanilla beans. If steeping any herbs or vanilla beans, add them when you take the pot off the heat. For herbs, add the leaves of a small bunch; for a vanilla bean, split the bean lengthwise, scrape the seeds into the sorbet mixture, and add the bean pod in. Glucose syrup is a common pastry ingredient, used to promote silky smooth textures and prevent crystallization; it's available online and perhaps at specialty grocers. (You can substitute half the amount of light corn syrup if need be, but the texture will be slightly different and the flavor will be sweeter.)

2 (13-ounce) cans coconut milk
2 (13-ounce) cans coconut cream
1¼ cups sugar
½ cup glucose syrup or corn syrup
1 teaspoon kosher salt

MAKES ABOUT 1 QUART

In a saucepan over medium-high heat, bring the coconut milk, coconut cream, sugar, glucose syrup, and salt to a simmer. When the sugar is fully dissolved, remove from the heat. Let sit covered in the refrigerator for 2 hours. Strain through a fine-mesh sieve and then churn in an ice cream machine as directed by manufacturer's instructions. (The sorbet can also be frozen and scraped with a fork, granita-style if you don't want to churn it in a machine.) Store in an airtight plastic container in the freezer indefinitely.

CHAPTER 8

CONDIMENTS AND BURGER PANTRY

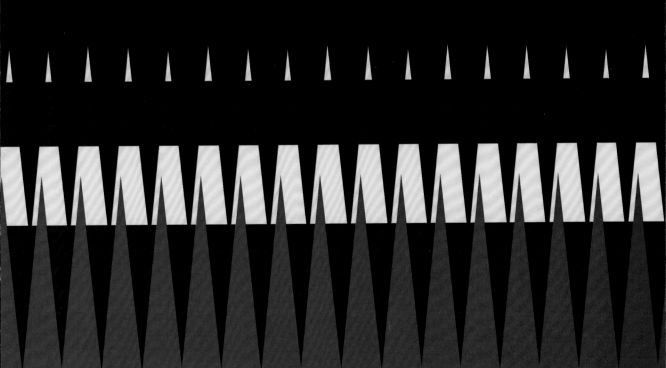

BASIC MAYO

There is a part of me that thinks we should have called Kronnerburger "MayonnaiseTown." I love mayonnaise. I love real, homemade mayonnaise, but I also love store-bought mayonnaise of every variety, with a particular soft spot for Duke's and Best Foods. Mayonnaise is the perfect sauce, and it works with both hot and cold foods. It's rich, it's salty, it's acidic. It's relatively easy to make, and there's nothing else like it. Plus, it's shelf-stable and will last for weeks. It's perfect. I love mayonnaise.

> 2 egg yolks
> ½ teaspoon kosher salt
> 1 teaspoon mustard powder
> 2 teaspoons distilled white vinegar
> 1½ cups neutral oil (such as safflower oil)
>
> **MAKES 1½ CUPS**

Combine the egg yolks, salt, mustard powder, and vinegar in a food processor and pulse until well combined, about 45 seconds. With the processor running, slowly add the oil and process until emulsified, about 3 minutes. Store in an airtight container in the refrigerator for 1 to 2 weeks.

CALABRIAN CHILE MAYONNAISE

Salt-cured Calabrian chiles are magic; not only do they pack a sharp, dry heat but they are loaded with more umami than just about any other preserved pepper. If you don't believe me, buy a jar and see how quickly you use them on everything—or end up eating them straight from the fridge.

Use this sauce, and its leftovers, for anything that you want to bathe in salty, spicy goodness: onion rings, french fries, grilled leeks, boiled eggs, and roasted potatoes or grilled shrimp, octopus, or any firm-fleshed seafood. If you can't get Calabrian chiles, pickled cherry peppers or rehydrated pasilla chiles also work pretty well.

> 2 egg yolks
> 1 large clove garlic, crushed with the side of your knife
> 1 tablespoon sherry vinegar
> 1 teaspoon liquid aminos
> ½ teaspoon kosher salt
> ½ teaspoon freshly ground black pepper
> ¼ teaspoon mustard powder
> ⅛ teaspoon Urfa, Marash, or Aleppo chile flakes
> 1½ cups neutral oil (such as safflower oil)
> ¼ cup oil-packed Calabrian chiles, drained and stemmed but not seeded
>
> **MAKES ABOUT 1½ CUPS; ENOUGH FOR A GROUP OF HUNGRY PEOPLE EATING ONION RINGS**

Combine the egg yolks, garlic, vinegar, liquid aminos, salt, pepper, mustard powder, and chile flakes in a food processor and process until combined. With the processor running, very slowly pour in 1 cup of the oil, almost at a drip, and then gradually increase the speed of the pour. If the oil starts to build up on the surface of the sauce, slow down the pour. The mixture will slowly thicken and ripples will form, as the mayonnaise's texture gradually builds.

When you've added the oil, add the chiles and process until well incorporated. The sauce will never really get smooth, so it's okay to keep some chile chunks. With the processor still running, pour in the remaining ½ cup oil and process until it reaches a consistency similar to mayonnaise. Store in an airtight container in the refrigerator for 1 to 2 weeks.

VEGAN "CHEDDAR" MAYONNAISE

Lecithins are the types of molecules used to bind cold emulsified sauces, such as mayonnaise and aioli. Lecithin is found in egg yolks, the usual ingredient in cold emulsifications made from scratch at home, but it's also found in soybeans. In fact, many commercial emulsifications use soy lecithin, not eggs, to create cheaper and more stable (and vegan) versions of mayonnaise.

There is no cheddar in this recipe, but it does have a similar flavor profile to the original. The nutritional yeast is a tried-and-true vegan cheat to add the richness of cheese.

> 1 cup soy milk
> 2 tablespoons sherry vinegar
> 2 tablespoons nutritional yeast
> 1 tablespoon mustard powder
> 1 teaspoon kosher salt
> 1 cup neutral oil (such as safflower oil)
>
> **MAKES 2 CUPS**

Combine the soy milk, vinegar, nutritional yeast, mustard powder, and salt in a blender or food processor and process until combined. With the processor running, slowly add the oil and process until it develops a thick, mayonnaise-like texture. Store in an airtight container in the refrigerator for 1 to 2 weeks.

QUICK MUSHROOM DIP

This dip is a quick, cooking-free version of the mushroom dip on page 136. Its smoothness is closer in heritage to an onion dip or cheese dip—but it's vegan. Serve cold with crudités, bread, pita, or chips.

> 1 cup soy milk
> 2 tablespoons sherry vinegar
> 2 tablespoons nutritional yeast
> 2 tablespoons onion powder
> 1 tablespoon mustard powder
> 1 teaspoon mushroom powder (see page 82)
> 1 teaspoon kosher salt
> 1 cup neutral oil (such as safflower oil)

SERVES 2 TO 4

Combine the soy milk, vinegar, nutritional yeast, onion powder, mustard powder, mushroom powder, and salt in a blender or food processer and process to combine. With the blender or processor running, very slowly pour in the oil, almost at a drip, and then gradually increase the speed of the pour. If the oil starts to build up on the surface of the sauce, slow down the pour. The mixture will slowly thicken and ripples will form, as the dip's texture gradually builds. Store in an airtight container indefinitely in the refrigerator.

TOFU MAYO

This recipe knows no limits; it's a workhorse, rich and unctuous but also relatively neutral. It works as a stand-alone sandwich topping as well as an excellent vegan base for dressings and other sauces.

The cashews are the key ingredient to fully round out the sauce, adding both unctuousness and texture. As such, unlike the other emulsified sauces, using a Vitamix or high-speed blender, not a food processor, really does make a difference to sufficiently smooth out the cashews to produce the right silky-smooth texture.

> 2 cups unsalted cashews
> ½ cup cider vinegar
> 1½ teaspoons kosher salt
> 1 teaspoon mustard powder
> 1½ cups neutral oil (such as safflower oil)
> 12 ounces firm tofu, coarsely chopped
> ¼ cup water or liquid from the tofu package

MAKES ABOUT 3 CUPS

Heat a sauté pan over medium heat. Add the cashews and toast until lightly browned, 3 to 4 minutes. Toss the nuts occasionally during toasting to be sure they don't burn. Remove from the heat and set aside.

In a Vitamix or other high-speed blender, combine the vinegar, salt, and mustard powder and process on low speed until combined. With the mixer running all the while, slowly add the oil and process until smooth and slightly thickened. Slowly add the still-warm nuts, increase the blender speed one level, and process until smooth. Add a handful of the tofu, process until smooth, and then increase the speed again to one more level. Add the remaining tofu in another two batches and process until smooth, using the blender's wand to push chunks off the sides of the blender and to ensure even consistency. Add the water and process until fluffy. The texture should be smooth, airy, and foamy—very similar to that of commercial mayonnaise. Store in an airtight container in the refrigerator for 1 to 2 weeks.

AIOLI

Just about every cook learns about emulsification through aioli. Especially when using a mortar and pestle, and you are constantly, feverishly working the sauce, aioli is the most visceral, straightforward, and connected way to understand how eggs and fats work together to create a unified whole. And it tastes amazing. Because of the olive oil and the garlic, it's a much more assertive sauce, yet the subtleties—the quality of oil, the amount of salt—can make a significant impact. I enjoy aioli with vegetables, shellfish, and just fries, or wherever mayonnaise is used.

> 2 egg yolks
> 2 cloves garlic, crushed with the side of your knife
> ½ teaspoon kosher salt
> Juice of 1 lemon
> ¾ cup extra-virgin olive oil

MAKES ¾ CUP

Combine the egg yolks, garlic, salt, and lemon juice in a food processor and process until smooth. With the processor running, slowly add the oil and process until emulsified, 1 to 2 minutes. Store in an airtight container in the refrigerator for up to 1 week.

RANCH DRESSING

Does ranch dressing need any justification or explanation?

> 2 egg yolks
> 6 large cloves garlic, crushed with the side of your knife
> ¼ cup cider vinegar
> 2 tablespoons onion powder
> 1 teaspoon ground fennel
> ½ teaspoon mustard powder
> ½ teaspoon celery seeds
> 1 bay leaf, finely chopped or ground
> 2 teaspoons freshly ground black pepper
> 1 teaspoon kosher salt
> 1 cup vegetable oil
> 1 bunch dill, leaves and thin stems
> 1 bunch flat-leaf parsley, leaves and thin stems
> ¼ cup crème fraîche

MAKES 1½ CUPS

Combine the egg yolks, garlic, vinegar, onion powder, ground fennel, mustard powder, celery seeds, bay leaf, pepper, and salt in a food processor and pulse to combine. With the processor running, slowly add ½ cup of the oil and process until well incorporated. Add the dill and parsley and pulse again until smooth and well incorporated, stirring if necessary. With the processor running, slowly add the remaining ½ cup of the oil until well incorporated. Add the crème fraîche and process until well incorporated. Store in an airtight container in the refrigerator for up to 2 weeks.

TARTAR SAUCE

A simple mixture of savory, tart, spicy, and creamy, tartar sauce is a great addition to your repertoire, especially as it pertains to its soul mate, fried seafood.

> 1 cup mayonnaise (page 216 or store-bought)
> 1 tablespoon diced pickled jalapeños
> 1 tablespoon diced dill pickles (page 64 or store-bought), plus 1 teaspoon dill pickle juice
> 1 teaspoon sugar
> 1 pinch of freshly ground black pepper
>
> **MAKES 1 CUP**

Stir together all of the ingredients in a bowl. Taste and adjust the seasoning. Store in an airtight container in the refrigerator for up to 1 week.

YUBA BACON

The time-consuming process of making yuba is a bit of an art. Very fresh soy milk is gently heated in large tanks until a thin film forms on the surface. This film is then removed in a sheet and that nearly transparent sheet of coagulated soy milk becomes yuba. When fully dried and fried, it has a texture similar to the lightest of chicharrones. I have found it to be a useful substitute for bacon on our vegetable-based sandwiches and burgers, like the Earth Burger (page 82). It also works well as a vegan and gluten-free delivery mechanism for dips and sauces.

> 1 thin (8-inch) sheet of fresh yuba
> 1 teaspoon paprika
> 1 teaspoon kosher salt
> ½ teaspoon sugar
> ¼ teaspoon freshly ground black pepper
> 1 pinch of ground allspice
> About 2 cups rice bran oil or other neutral oil, or as needed to submerge the yuba
>
> **MAKES 4 STRIPS, ENOUGH FOR ONE BATCH OF EARTH BURGERS (PAGE 82)**

Unfold the yuba, if necessary, into a single flat sheet, trying not to tear it as you do so. Slice into 4-inch squares and lay out on a baking sheet or plate. Let dry at room temperature for at least 6 hours, or up to overnight.

In a small bowl, combine and mix the paprika, salt, sugar, pepper, and allspice. Set aside.

In a cast-iron pan or heavy pot, heat the oil to 385°F over high heat. Working in batches, fry the yuba until it puffs and becomes golden and crisp. Adjust the heat as needed to maintain the oil temperature at 375°F. Using a spider skimmer or other small strainer, remove the yuba from the oil and drain on paper towels. Season with the spice blend. Eat immediately.

AMERICAN CHEESE

For a saucy version of this recipe—because who doesn't love a good cheese sauce—substitute the gelatin and hot water with a slurry made of 1 tablespoon cornstarch and 2 tablespoons tap water.

⅓ cup evaporated milk

1 tablespoon powdered plain gelatin

2 tablespoons hot water

1 teaspoon mustard powder

½ teaspoon kosher salt

5 ounces cheddar cheese, grated

MAKES ½ POUND

Heat the evaporated milk in a saucepan over medium-high heat until it simmers. Meanwhile, put the gelatin in a small bowl and add the hot water to prompt it to bloom. When the milk simmers, add the gelatin mixture, mustard powder, and salt and stir to combine. Add the cheese and whisk until smooth. Once smooth and well incorporated, pour the mixture into a terrine mold, rimmed baking dish, or similar container that is lined with plastic wrap. Let cool. Once fully cooled, cut into thin slices. It will keep unsliced for weeks in plastic wrap in the refrigerator. Store in plastic wrap in the refrigerator for up to 2 weeks.

CHILE OIL

This fiery chile oil is good for almost anything: on tartare, over eggs or raw fish, mixed with rice, on simple roasted vegetables, for self-defense. Mix it with cold leftover chicken, potatoes, and nuts for an easy salad. And since this is a hamburger book, you can also pour it all over a hamburger.

2 cups neutral oil (such as safflower oil)

6 cloves garlic, minced

⅓ cup onion powder

⅓ cup red pepper flakes

⅓ cup Urfa, Marash, or Aleppo chile flakes

¼ cup black peppercorns

1 teaspoon white peppercorns

1 teaspoon allspice berries

¼ cup soy sauce

MAKES 3 CUPS

In a small saucepan, heat the oil to 240°F over medium heat. Add the garlic and fry until it is lightly cooked, about 2 minutes, being careful not to brown it. Add the onion powder, red pepper flakes, chile flakes, black peppercorns, white peppercorns, and allspice berries and cook until lightly fragrant, about 5 minutes. Adjust the heat as needed to maintain the oil temperature at 225°F. You want the spices to cook, not fry; don't let them darken or smoke. When everything is nice and fragrant, remove from the heat. Stir in the soy sauce and let cool. Store in an airtight container in the refrigerator indefinitely.

QUICK PICKLED CHILES

Fast, easy, and versatile, this pickle recipe can be used for most vegetables cut to a similar size as the peppers used here, such as onions or green tomatoes. But it's best with chiles, especially spicy ones like Fresnos and jalapeños, to give any sandwich or salad an extra bite.

8 ounces Fresno chiles, jalapeño chiles, or (for a non-spicy option) banana peppers

1 cup rice vinegar

1 tablespoon kosher salt

1 teaspoon dill seeds

½ teaspoon fenugreek seeds

**MAKES 1 TO 2 CUPS OF PICKLES;
ENOUGH FOR SEVERAL ROUNDS OF BURGERS**

Cut the tops off the chiles and slice the chiles into ⅛-inch rounds. Put the chiles in a sealable jar or bowl.

Combine the rice vinegar, salt, dill seeds, and fenugreek seeds in a small saucepan and bring to a boil over high heat.

Meanwhile, prepare an ice bath.

Pour the boiling vinegar mixture over the chiles. Make sure the chiles are completely submerged, weighing them down with another container if necessary. Put the container in the ice bath and refrigerate for 30 minutes before eating. Store peppers submerged in the brine in the refrigerator indefinitely.

BREAD AND BUTTER PICKLES

Just as the Patty Melt (page 74) is the Kronnerburger's nemesis, so is the bread and butter pickle the shadow self of the dill pickle. Whereas the dill pickle is all about salt, acidity, crispness, and forceful restraint, the bread and butter pickle is fuzzy, bright, luscious, all embracing, and buttery.

1½ pounds pickling cucumbers, green tomatoes, or zucchini

2 tablespoons kosher salt

1 small white onion, quartered through the root end

2 cloves garlic

2 tablespoons sugar

2 tablespoons coriander seeds

1 tablespoon plus 1 teaspoon caraway seeds

1 tablespoon fenugreek seeds

1 tablespoon ground turmeric

1 tablespoon black peppercorns

2 teaspoons mustard seeds

1½ teaspoons anise seeds, or 1 star anise pod

1 teaspoon fennel seeds

½ teaspoon celery seeds

8 whole cloves

4 allspice berries

2 bay leaves

2 cups distilled white vinegar

MAKES 1 QUART

Wash the cucumbers well. Trim off and discard the ends and cut into ¼-inch slices. Put the slices into a 1-quart sealable plastic container or mason jar. Add the salt and toss to evenly distribute.

Heat a pot over medium heat. Combine the onion, garlic, sugar, coriander seeds, caraway seeds, fenugreek seeds, turmeric, peppercorns, mustard seeds, anise seeds, fennel seeds, celery

CONTINUED

seeds, cloves, allspice berries, and bay leaves in the pot and toast until fragrant, about 1 minute. Toss often during toasting to be sure they don't burn. Add the vinegar, turn the heat to high, and bring to a simmer. Once the vinegar mixture reaches a simmer, remove from the heat and let cool for 5 minutes.

Prepare an ice bath that can fit the base of the pickle container.

Take a foot-long square of cheesecloth and drape it over the top of the pickle container to create a strainer. Pour the hot vinegar mixture, including the sugar, spices, onion, and garlic, through the cheesecloth and into the jar with the cucumbers. The cheesecloth should catch the spices. Twist the corners of the cheesecloth together to turn it into a spice-filled bundle that will sit in the brine atop the cucumbers. You want the spices to be in the brine but filtered out from the vegetables. If necessary, tie the cheesecloth bundle up with kitchen twine.

Make sure the cucumbers on the bottom are completely submerged in the brine by shaking the container and stirring the contents if necessary. Put the container—with the spice bundle—in the ice bath and let cool. Once cooled, the pickles are ready to eat. Store in the refrigerator indefinitely.

LACTO-FERMENTED PICKLES

I love the taste and texture of wild-fermented pickles. They ignite memories of the deli sandwiches and the diner hamburgers and the Coney Island hot dogs of my Michigan youth. There is a certain amount of variability inherent in this type of fermentation, which has kept me from using it for the pickles at the restaurant. At the end of the day, vinegar processes are more controllable and quicker, but nothing compares to the wild taste of an old-timey dill pickle.

Whereas the quick pickle recipes can use plastic containers if necessary, this one really does require a sanitized glass gallon mason jar.

> 3 pounds pickling cucumbers, or as many as can fit in your jar
>
> ½ cup loose-leaf black tea leaves
>
> 1 tablespoon dill seeds
>
> ½ teaspoon celery seeds
>
> 1 tablespoon plus 1 teaspoon caraway seeds
>
> 4 whole cloves
>
> 1½ teaspoons anise seeds, or 1 star anise pod
>
> 1 tablespoon black peppercorns
>
> 1 teaspoon fennel seeds
>
> 2 teaspoons mustard seeds
>
> 2 tablespoons coriander seeds
>
> 4 allspice berries
>
> 2 bay leaves
>
> 1 bunch dill
>
> 6 cloves garlic
>
> 1 small white onion, quartered through the root end
>
> 10 tablespoons fine sea salt
>
> 4 quarts nonchlorinated water

MAKES 1 GALLON OF WHOLE PICKLES

Thoroughly wash the cucumbers. Trim off and discard the ends. In a large mason jar, combine the cucumbers with all the other ingredients except the salt and water.

In a separate vessel, combine the salt and water and mix until the salt is dissolved. Pour into the cucumber jar until all the cucumbers are fully submerged, using a clean plate to weigh down the cucumbers and make sure they are all submerged. Put on the lid. Leave in a cool space for 1 week, and then transfer to the refrigerator. Will keep in the refrigerator for several weeks.

CHAD'S SOURDOUGH LEAVEN

A slightly shorter version of the *Tartine Bread* version, this starter is the basis for Chad's brioche buns (recipe follows) and the Pullman Loaf Levain (page 231). In short, a starter is a magical ingredient that adds flavor and complexity to bread. The process takes several days and then needs to be maintained periodically. First, you have to create a culture from flour and water, which then ferments. Once fermentation begins, you feed the culture and then it becomes your starter.

> 625 grams (4 cups) white bread flour
> 625 grams (4 cups) whole wheat bread flour
> Water

Make a 50/50 blend: In a large bowl, mix the two flours. This will be the blend that you use to fed your culture and develop your starter.

Make the starter: In a medium bowl, place 300 grams (about 1⅓ cup) of slightly warm (80°F to 85°F) water. Add one-quarter of the 50/50 flour blend (reserve the remaining flour blend), and mix with your hand or a wooden spoon to combine until the mixture is free of any dry bits. Cover the mixture with a clean, dry kitchen towel or cheesecloth and let stand at a warm room temperature until bubbles start to form around the sides and on the surface, about 2 days. It's important to maintain a warm temperature. Let stand another day to allow fermentation to progress a bit. More bubbles should form. This is your starter. It will smell acidic and slightly funky. At this stage it's time to train your starter into a leaven by feeding it fresh flour and water at regular intervals.

Feed the starter: Transfer about an eighth of the starter—about 75 grams—to a clean bowl and discard the remainder of the starter. To the 75 grams of starter, add 150 grams (about 1 cup) of the 50/50 blend and 150 grams (about ⅔ cup) warm (80°F to 85°F) water. Mix to combine; it should have the consistency of pancake batter. Repeat this feeding process once every 24 hours at the same time of day, always transferring 75 grams of the starter to a clean bowl and discarding the remainder, then adding the flour and water and re-covering the bowl with a clean, dry kitchen towel after each feeding and letting the mixture stand at warm room temperature. The batter should start to rise and fall consistently throughout the day after a few days of feedings. As the starter develops, the smell will change from ripe and sour to sweet and pleasantly fermented, like yogurt. Once this sweet lactic character is established and the fermentation is predictable, a few days to one week, it's time to make the leaven from this mature starter.

Make the leaven: The leaven is the portion of prefermented flour and water that will go into your final bread dough and raise the whole mass. Two days before you want to make bread, feed the matured starter twice daily, once in the morning and once in the evening, to increase fermentation activity. When you are ready to make the dough, discard all but 1 tablespoon of the matured starter. To the remaining 1 tablespoon, add 200 grams (about 1¼ cup) of the 50/50 flour blend and 200 grams (about 1 cup) warm (80°F to 85°F) water. This is your leaven. Cover and let rest at moderate room temperature for 4 to 6 hours.

To test the leaven's readiness, drop a spoonful into a bowl of room temperature water. If it sinks, it is not ready and needs more time to ripen. When it floats on the surface or close to it, it's ready to use.

To maintain the leaven for regular use, continue feeding daily as described earlier.

BRIOCHE BUN

This is Chad's bun recipe, used with permission and love. If nothing else, it should give you an appreciation for all that goes into good bread, let alone great bread like that from Tartine. Brioche dough freezes well if you want to reserve some of the buns to bake another day.

POOLISH

1⅔ cups (200 grams) all-purpose flour
1 cup (236 grams) warm water
1 tablespoon (13 grams) active dry yeast
Chad's Sourdough Leaven (page 225)

DOUGH

2 cups (450 grams) unsalted butter
7¼ cups (1 kilogram) bread flour
⅔ cup (120 grams) sugar
3 tablespoons (25 grams) kosher salt
3¼ teaspoons (10 grams) active dry yeast
10 eggs (500 grams)
1 cup (240 grams) whole milk

EGG WASH

2 egg yolks
1 tablespoon heavy cream
1 tablespoon poppy seeds
1 teaspoon sesame seeds

MAKES 12 BUNS

To make the poolish: The night before you want to bake, stir together the flour, water, and yeast in a bowl. Let stand overnight in the refrigerator.

The next morning, drop a spoonful each of the poolish and leaven into a bowl of water. If they float, they're ready. If they don't, they need more time to ferment. Check back in 1 hour.

To make the dough: About 30 minutes before you are ready to mix the dough, remove the butter from the refrigerator and let soften at room temperature until pliable but cool.

Attach the dough hook to a stand mixer. Put the flour, sugar, salt, and yeast in the mixing bowl. Add the eggs, milk, leaven, and poolish and mix on low speed until combined, 3 to 5 minutes. Scrape down the bowl and let the dough rest for 15 to 20 minutes.

Mix the dough again on medium speed until it releases from the sides of the bowl, 6 to 8 minutes.

Cut the butter into ½-inch pieces. With the mixer on medium speed, add the butter, one piece at a time, to the middle of the bowl. Continue to mix until all the butter is incorporated.

Transfer the dough to a bowl and set in a cool spot for 2 hours to ferment. Every hour, grab the underside of the dough and pull it up to the surface. After 2 hours, freeze or bake the dough.

At least 3 hours before serving the burgers, portion the dough into 4-ounce (115-gram) pieces, each the size of a large plum, and form the dough into bun shapes. Place the buns on a baking sheet, spacing them 6 inches apart. Press slightly to flatten and spread them a bit. Let rise at moderate room temperature for 1½ to 2 hours, until doubled in height.

Preheat the oven to 450°F.

To make the egg wash: Stir together the egg yolks and heavy cream in a small bowl.

Using a pastry brush, lightly brush the buns with the egg wash and sprinkle with the poppy seeds and sesame seeds. Bake until the buns are golden brown, about 15 minutes. Let cool before slicing for burgers. The buns are best enjoyed when baked and eaten on the same day.

VEGAN BUN

This is the vegan version of our bun. The dairy and egg are replaced with olive oil. When we first opened the restaurant, we decided that if we were going to go through the effort to make a vegan patty as well as other vegan food, it was necessary to offer vegan buns for a fully vegan version of the Earth Burger (page 82).

3¾ cups (486 grams) all-purpose flour

1¼ cups (297 grams) water

3 tablespoons plus 1 teaspoon (45 grams) extra-virgin olive oil

3 tablespoons (35 grams) sugar

2 tablespoons plus 2 teaspoons (27 grams) potato flour

1¾ teaspoons (9 grams) kosher salt

2¼ teaspoons (9 grams) yeast

BUN WASH

1 tablespoon cornstarch

1 cup water

1 tablespoon nigella seeds (optional)

MAKES 12 BUNS

In a mixing bowl fitted with the hook attachment, combine the all-purpose flour, water, oil, sugar, potato flour, salt, and yeast and mix for 7 minutes on the lowest speed. Scrape your bowl and mix for another 7 minutes, this time on the next highest speed.

Transfer the dough to a covered container and let rest for at least 12 hours, or up to overnight.

After resting, divide the dough into twelve portions, each the size of a large plum, about 2½ ounces (70 grams). Line a baking sheet with greased parchment paper.

Working with one piece of dough at a time on a lightly floured work surface, roll the dough into balls. To form tight, smooth, perfect balls, connect your thumb and index finger and form a "cage"—your thumb and the edge of your pinkie should be the boundaries—and roll the ball into the corner of your hand to force the edges below the round of dough. Your buns should have a smooth exposed surface if rolled correctly. Arrange the dough portions with 1 inch between them on the prepared baking sheet and allow to proof for 1 hour.

Once the dough has proofed, flatten it gently into 4-inch rounds, and let rest again at room temperature until it's puffy and springs back slowly.

Preheat the oven to 425°F.

To make the bun wash: Boil the cornstarch and water in a small pan over high heat. Brush the wash onto the dough buns and then sprinkle with the nigella seeds.

Once the oven has reached temperature, put one or two oven-safe containers—cast-iron pans work great—on the bottom rack and fill with ice cubes or water. The goal here is to create a steamy environment in the oven to ensure a nice, crusty outer layer. Let steam for 10 minutes. Refill the water and at the same time, put in the buns. Bake for 18 minutes, until the buns are golden brown. Let cool before slicing for burgers. Keep covered at room temperature for 2 to 3 days. If storing longer, freeze. Can be frozen up to 1 month.

GLUTEN-FREE BUN

The first time we used these gluten-free buns was in conjunction with Earth Burgers (page 82), and guests were surprised—but not disappointed—to discover that the patties were not meat and that the buns were free of gluten.

We use Cup4Cup—a gluten-free flour developed by a former pastry chef from the French Laundry—and have found that it produces excellent gluten-free baked goods. This dough does not look, feel, or behave like a normal wheat-based bread dough. It is relatively wet and needs to be handled gently. It is also important to not allow the buns to proof for too long, as that will result in buns that will not hold their shape and integrity when baked.

 1 tablespoon plus 2 teaspoons (20 grams) active dry yeast

 1¼ cups (296 grams) warm water

 3 cups (418 grams) gluten-free flour (see Note, page 230), plus more for sprinkling

 ⅓ cup (81 grams) packed brown sugar

 ⅓ cup (81 grams) lightly beaten eggs

 3 tablespoons (40 grams) unsalted butter

 ⅓ cup (40 grams) milk powder

 1¾ teaspoons (10 grams) kosher salt

 2 teaspoons (10 grams) cider vinegar

 1 tablespoon (10 grams) xanthan gum

EGG WASH

 1 egg

 ¼ cup water

 1 pinch of kosher salt

 1 tablespoon sesame seeds

MAKES 10 BUNS

Combine the yeast and warm water in a small bowl and let sit for 10 to 15 minutes. The yeast is active when bubbles can be seen on the surface of the mixture.

Combine the flour, brown sugar, eggs, butter, milk powder, salt, vinegar, and xanthan gum in the bowl of a stand mixer fitted with the paddle and mix on low speed. Turn the speed to medium and mix for 5 minutes to aerate. Put the dough in an oiled bowl and let rise until slightly puffy, about 30 minutes at room temperature. Don't wait too long, because gluten-free dough will not proof a second time after it has deflated.

CONTINUED

Coat a clean surface with nonstick cooking spray and sprinkle heavily with gluten-free flour. The dough will be very wet, so be patient and don't be afraid to add more flour.

Using a rolling pin well-dusted with gluten-free flour, gently flatten the dough so it is uniformly and evenly about ¾ inch thick. Cut out circles that are 3½ inches in diameter with an oiled and floured cutter. Arrange on baking sheets and move to a rack to proof (it does not need to be covered rack) for 20 to 40 minutes. When the buns have puffed up and stay indented when you poke them, they're ready to bake.

Meanwhile, preheat the oven to 400°F.

To make the egg wash: Combine the egg, water, and salt in a small bowl and whisk to mix.

When the buns are ready to bake, brush them with the egg wash and sprinkle with sesame seeds.

Once the oven has reached temperature, put one or two oven-safe containers—cast-iron pans work great—on the bottom rack and fill with ice cubes or water. The goal here is to create a steamy environment in the oven to ensure a nice, crusty outer layer. Let steam for 10 minutes. Refill the water and at the same time, put in the buns. Bake for 10 minutes, until the buns are golden brown. Let cool before slicing for burgers. Keep covered at room temperature for 2 to 3 days. They will keep, frozen, for up to a month.

Note: The volume measurement of the flour may vary based on brand, so weigh the flour if possible.

BISCUITS

These biscuits are so buttery and flaky that they are practically croissants. Use them in place of a bun, with your favorite burger patty, or on their own with butter and jam.

> 3½ cups (450 grams) all-purpose flour, or as needed
>
> 1 tablespoon (12 grams) sugar
>
> 1 tablespoon plus ¼ teaspoon (15 grams) baking powder
>
> 1¼ teaspoons (7 grams) kosher salt
>
> ½ teaspoon (3 grams) baking soda
>
> 1¼ cups (280 grams) cold butter
>
> 1¼ cups (310 grams) buttermilk, plus more for brushing

MAKES 8 BISCUITS

In a large bowl, combine the flour, sugar, baking powder, salt, and baking soda. Sift onto a clean work surface, like a table or big cutting board.

Cut the cold butter into ⅛-inch slices. Working one piece at a time, press the butter with the heel of your hand into the dry ingredients; ribbons of flour and butter should be formed as you combine the butter and flour mixture. Repeat until all the butter is fully incorporated. Using your hands, gently incorporate the buttermilk until just combined. The dough should be handled as little as possible and not kneaded or overmixed.

Form the mixture into a rectangle about 16 by 12 inches. Using a rolling pin in only one direction (that is, repeatedly roll only one way; don't go back and forth), flatten the square until the thickness is ¾ to 1 inch. Add minimal amounts of flour if the dough is sticking. Cover in plastic wrap and refrigerate for 15 minutes.

Now it's time to laminate. Using the rolling pin—again, moving only in a single direction—roll out the dough, pushing it out until it is doubled in length, adding minimal flour as necessary to prevent sticking. Fold the new extension back onto the dough, re-forming the original rectangle. Rotate the dough 90 degrees and repeat. Rolling the dough forward until doubled in size and folding it back over itself. Place in the refrigerator for 20 minutes. The resting component is very important to prevent the biscuits from becoming tough. Repeat the rolling, folding, and resting processes another two times. When done correctly, the resulting biscuits will be wonderfully flaky.

Cover the dough with plastic wrap and freeze for 30 minutes. Preheat the oven to 425°F.

Cut the dough into 3-inch squares and arrange on a baking sheet, at least 1 inch apart. Using a pastry brush, brush additional buttermilk over the squares. Bake for 30 minutes, until the biscuits are golden brown. Eat immediately.

PULLMAN LOAF LEVAIN

The Pullman loaf is ideal for sandwiches; it is baked in a long narrow pan, resulting in a familiar Wonder Bread shape. Hence, you will need a Pullman loaf pan. This bread, which is a blend of rye, sourdough, and good old-fashioned white bread, is exceptional when sliced for patty melts (page 74) or Reubens, or used a vehicle for toast toppings.

3¾ cups (516 grams) bread flour
1⅓ cups (163 grams) durum flour
3 tablespoons (22 grams) graham flour
⅓ cup (37 grams) rye flour
2½ cups (592 grams) plus 1 tablespoon (15 grams) warm water

½ cup (132 grams) sourdough leaven (page 225)
1 tablespoon (18 grams) kosher salt
Butter, for greasing

MAKES 1 LOAF

In a large bowl, mix the bread flour, durum flour, graham flour, and rye flour.

Pour the 2½ cups (592 grams) water into the bowl of a stand mixer fitted with the hook attachment. Add the sourdough starter. The starter must float. If it doesn't float, wait until it does, or revive it by feeding it, or put it somewhere warm to activate it more quickly. Mix on low speed until combined. With the mixer still running, slowly add the flour mixture. When thoroughly combined, scrape down the sides of the bowl. Mix again for 2 minutes more, until the dough is well combined. It should be shaggy and sticky, wet but still with structure. Let sit for 30 minutes. (This step is called the autolyse.)

After 30 minutes, mix the dough on low speed for 4 minutes. The dough should feel fluffy and soft, not tight and dry. Once dough has reached that desired consistency, add the salt with the remaining 1 tablespoon (15 grams) water. Mix on low speed until incorporated, then increase to the next highest speed and mix for 2 minutes. While the dough mixes, prepare a large, lightly greased bowl or dough tub. Transfer the dough from the mixer to the bowl. Cover with a cloth towel, and let rest for 2 hours, until the volume has increased by 30 percent.

During these 2 hours of the dough's rest/rise, gently turn the dough every 30 minutes—bring the dough on the bottom to the top, trying not to deflate the dough and losing too much of the air.

CONTINUED

Condiments and Burger Pantry

Once dough volume has increased by 30 percent after 2 hours, transfer from the bowl to a clean work surface, like a table or large cutting board. Let sit for 20 minutes.

Meanwhile, preheat the oven to 500°F and grease your Pullman loaf pan with butter.

After the dough rests for 20 minutes, it's time to shape it. Making sure to handle the dough carefully and taking care not to expel the gases, gently form it into a rough rectangle. Working one at a time, grab each corner and drag it to the center of the dough; forming a loglike shape that will fit in the pan. Once all the corners are "connected" in the middle, flip the dough upside down into the pan, so the surface that was facing you is now facedown in the pan. Let proof at room temperature until the dough reaches the top of the pan. (If you're not baking right away, refrigerate for up to 12 hours; if your dough was refrigerated, let it sit at room temperature for 30 minutes before baking.)

Once the oven has reached temperature, put one or two oven-safe containers—cast-iron pans work great—one the bottom rack and fill with ice cubes or water. The goal here is to create a steamy environment in the oven to ensure a nice, crusty outer bread layer. Let steam for 10 minutes. Refill the water and at the same time, put in the bread and then lower the temperature to 475°F. Bake for 45 minutes, or until the bread has an internal temperature of 205°F. Remove from the oven and turn out of the pan. Let cool before eating.

Keep covered at room temperature for 2 to 3 days. It will keep frozen for up to 1 month.

ACKNOWLEDGMENTS

Thank you to **Donna** and **Joe**, my parents, for not succumbing to frustration and suffocating me. Allowing me to live and choosing not to kill me at various points throughout the past thirty-five years has made so many hamburgers possible. Thank you both. Thank you **Bill** (my mother's husband) and **Lisa** (my father's wife) for supporting your respective spouses and myself. I love you guys dearly. The past six years, this book, and Kronnerburger could not have happened without my wife **Ashley** and our son **Jim**. When Ashley and I met I was basically homeless and unemployed, but I had an idea. She was intelligent, ambitious, kind, beautiful, and extremely capable. It was my need to impress her (and a desire for shelter and some money) that motivated me to turn that idea into my current, ever-evolving hamburger reality. Without her vision, hard work, and superior grip on the present I would most likely still be homeless and would not have such a handsome son. I moved to Northern California in 2001. My dear friend, culinary school classmate, and Tartine bakery employee **Wendy Muster** introduced me to **Chad Robertson** and **Elisabeth Prueitt**. Chad and Liz have been my landlords, employers, best critics, and most importantly, mentors for fifteen years. They are two of the most talented and generous people I have ever encountered. My life in California and all of the time I have spent in kitchens would not have happened without the two of them and their guidance, support, and influence. I love you both (and Archer too) and cannot ever fully express how grateful I am for the two of you. **Steven** and **Mitch Rosenthal**, **Johnny Nunn**, **Paul**, and **Jason** put up with me for nearly two years at Town Hall in San Francisco and I thank them for the BBQ shrimp–related nightmares that haunt my sleep (and for **Mary's** advice on the importance of a correctly dressed salad). If **Charles Phan** had not thought me too young to be a sous chef at the Slanted Door, **Justine Kelly** would not have sent me to work for **Sante Salvoni** at the best San Francisco neighborhood restaurant ever, the Slow Club. Sante let me be his sous chef and for that I will be forever grateful. He is the original reluctant burger master. Sante encouraged me to be creative, taught me more than I can list, and showed me the importance of the kitchen's relationship with the farmers, fishermen, and ranchers who supply our food. He is still the best cook I know. I love you, Chef. Well done burger, well done bun. **Erin Rooney** took a second chance on me when she made me the chef of the Slow Club. She effortlessly ran a place that was both incredibly warm and endlessly cool. She allowed me the freedom and gentle guidance needed to understand what makes a restaurant great. She gave me confidence for the first time in my career. Thank you Erin, for your patience and for believing in me. I owe **Samantha Strand** endless thanks for giving life to all of the weirdness that is Kronnerburger's visual identity. You are a brilliant wild creature. Thank you for challenging me, very rarely saying no, and being the best kind of friend a burger boy could ask for. Old Western Town for life. **Paolo Lucchesi**, you are a better writer, communicator, husband, and father than I could hope to become. Thank you for questioning everything and constantly pushing—occasionally dragging— us in the right direction. You have made this book, my food, and myself much improved having known you. Thank you for your dedication and companionship. **Eric Wolfinger** has been called the LeBron James of food photography by the newspaper of record. I like to think of Eric as LeBron when we talk on the phone and he explains to me why everything is going to work out. Your professionalism, inspiring hair, and skill with a camera never cease to inspire me. Thank you for many years of friendship and stepping out of the box to make this book happen. **Jenny Wapner** may, on occasion, regret approaching me about writing a cookbook nearly two years ago. I imagine she often wished she had asked literally anyone else. Despite my not-exactly-linear process since that first meeting, Jenny kept us on track and patiently coaxed me into making something that hopefully more than one person reads. There is still time for her to punch me in the face. Even if she eventually punches me, I want to thank her and the entire team at Ten Speed for giving this book life. Thank you to **Aaron**, **Emily**, **Emma**, **Serena**, **Mari**, **Lisa**, and **Kara**. **Katherine Cowles** is the most diplomatic person I know. Were she not already the best agent, heading the State Department might be a fitting alternative. Thank you for your faith, wisdom, and for believing in my burger. Thank you to **Sam** (artist), **Howie** (poet), **Christa**, **Danny**, and everyone else from that cheetah-print-carpeted room on Mission Street where the burger began to form. To sweet **William "Billy" Niles**, cool dad, longtime kitchen companion, and creative inspiration both at Bar Tartine and Kronnerburger. Hardest working gentleman I know. **Ethan Mitchel** and **Oliver Monday**, original burger boys, from sour man village to sweet boy city. **David Cabello**, my first San Francisco friend. Scamp. **Andrew Mariani** creator of cool wine, Eagle. **Kevin Cimino**, burger cuisinist, friend to rabbits, stunt drive co-pilot, Kronner caretaker. **Adam Hatch**, original Kronnerburger patron, hamburger artist, real world domain host. **Bradford Taylor**, the most generous king of the juice, salami party enthusiast, inspired money loser. **Reginaldo Sontay**, the man who has made more Kronnerburgers than anyone on earth. **Kevin Swanberg**, the man who has eaten more Kronner-burgers than anyone on earth. **Andrew Tarlow** for being my NY home and constantly reminding me that art is life and life is an art. **Gabriel Lowe**, margarita master. **Alex** and **Brack**, my two dads. **Wylie Price**, originator of Snuff Milk. Original Kronnerburger crew: **Ashley**, **Sante**, **Gabriel**, **Swanberg**, **Brandon**, **Lisa Marie**, **Cassie**, **David**, **Betty**, **Alex**, **Brack**, **Wayne**, **Christa**, **Cogan**, **Zeina**, **Cat**, **Bondick**, **Jacob**, **Paul**, **Hannah**, **Hasti**, **Anna**, **Fitch**, **Kevin**. **Daniel Duane** is the most dedicated burger enthusiast around, testing every wild idea on his unsuspecting family. I am so happy we encountered one another and that I have your most inquisitive mind as a resource. Thank you for your endless enthusiasm and brilliant writing. **Chris Fischer** and **Julia Sherman**. Thank you for your wisdom, listening to me blather, and sharing the experiences that make you both so talented and singular. **Lee** and **Anna**, each masters of their respective realms. **Harold McGee**. **Helen** and **John** at Vice. **Andrew**, **Lilli**, and everyone at *Bon Appétit*. **Cal Peternell**. **Kim Hastreiter**. **Jane White**, my second mom and original Kronnerburger investor. **Nicole** and **Justin** and the things to come. Everyone that has hosted Kronnerburger over the years: **Dennis**, **David**, and **Dan Lee** from Namu. **Danny Newberg** of Joint Venture. **Scott**, **Josh**, and **Morgan** at Trick Dog. **Jeremy**, **Tal**, **Jodi**, and **Josie** of FourBarrel/The Mill. **Vinny** at Tartine. **Charlie** at Pizzaiolo. **Rimpei** at Pignon. **Ari** at Alma. **Yoko** and **Kayoko** at Umami Mart. **Jessica** and **Javier** at Sqirl. **Nick**, **Gabe**, and **Bobby** at GG's. **Marc** from Burger Records. **Suzanne Drexhage** at Bartavelle. **Patrick** and **Cheryln** at Tank 18. **David** and **Steven** at Shibumi. **Carl Sutton** of Sutton Cellars. **Jason** at Bar Bandini. **Oscar** and **Jake** of Tacos Oscar. **Erik**, **Todd**, and **Ryan** of ABV. **Jessica Silverman** of Silverman Gallery. **David**, **Erin**, and **Michael** at Minnesota Street Project. **Karen** and **Rachel** at Mercy. **Jon Santer** and **Dylan O'Brien** of Prizefighter. **Adam Katz** of Imprint. **Dave Gould** and **Sean Rembold**, the owners of Achilles Heel. **Bradford Taylor** of Ordinaire. **Ruth** and **Peter** at Lawton Trading Post. **Creative Growth**. **Jane White**, my second mom and original Kronnerburger investor. **Rick Howard** and **Hal Brandel**, endlessly patient supporters. **Todd** and **Jodie**. **Alex** and **Tony**. Thank you to my many meat friends who have shaped the burger over the years: **Bill Niman**, **Cliff "The Mandarin" Pollard**, **Ryan Farr**, **Taylor Boetticher**, **Sasha Wizansky**, **Mac Magruder**, **Mark Pasternak**, **Doug Stonebreaker**, **Loren Poncia**, and **Claire Herminjard**.

INDEX

Text copyright © 2018 by Chris Kronner
Photographs copyright © 2018 by Eric Wolfinger
Illustrations copyright © 2018 by Samantha Strand

Published in the United States by Ten Speed Press, an imprint
of the Crown Publishing Group, a division of Penguin Random
House LLC, New York.
www.crownpublishing.com
www.tenspeed.com

Ten Speed Press and the Ten Speed Press colophon are registered
trademarks of Penguin Random House LLC.

Library of Congress Cataloging-in-Publication Data is on file
with the publisher.

Hardcover ISBN: 978-0-399-57926-4
eBook ISBN: 978-0-399-57927-1

Printed in China

Design by Emma Campion

10 9 8 7 6 5 4 3 2

First Edition